D1765796

C016132328

Clear Your House

First published in 2015 by New Holland Publishers Pty Ltd
London · Sydney · Auckland
www.newhollandpublishers.com

The Chandlery Unit 009, 50 Westminster Bridge Road, London SE1 7QY,
United Kingdom
1/66 Gibbes Street, Chatswood, NSW 2067, Australia
5/39 Woodside Ave, Northcote, Auckland 0627, New Zealand

ISBN: 9781742576695

Managing Director: Fiona Schultz
Publisher: Diane Ward
Editor: Anna Brett
Design: Andrew Quinlan
Production Director: Olga Dementiev
Printer: Toppan Leefung (China) Ltd
10 9 8 7 6 5 4 3 2 1

Keep up with New Holland Publishers on Facebook
www.facebook.com/NewHollandPublishers

CONTENTS

INTRODUCTION

What Is Space Clearing?

'Space clearing' is a term used to energetically transform a space or area that may have some stagnant, heavy or dull energy attached to it. There are various tools and techniques that can be used to lift the energy in an area to create harmony, balance and to restore the positive energy.

Energetic space clearing is not a new concept, it has been around for thousands of years, it is an ancient spiritual technique that is practiced around the world by people from many different religions and cultures. For example, some Indigenous Australian tribes burn eucalyptus leaves and use clap sticks and some Native Americans burn sage, cedar and sweet grass with the use of rattles and drums to space clear an area. In some Asian countries such as China, Thailand, Tibet and Bali they use incense, bells, gongs and chanting to clear a space, whilst in some Western Christian religions church bells, incense, prayers and holy water are used to clear negative energy.

There are many cultures who each have their own unique methods and tools to space clear. It doesn't matter what the differences are amongst the cultures, they all have one thing in common, they all want to clear out the old, negative energy in a space to make it more balanced, positive and protected for the people that live in or visit that space.

CHAPTER 1

WHEN SHOULD YOU SPACE CLEAR?

Emotional And Physical Signs

Energy is everywhere, it is connected to people, objects, buildings, spaces and environments. Even though you can't see energy with your physical eyes you can definitely feel it physically around you. An example of this is when you walk into a crowded room and you feel the group's energy is stressed or something strange has happened just before you arrived. After you question people about how they are, they admit that earlier in the room there was a fight between two people, this happened just before you arrived. This shows how you can feel energy without seeing it.

Another example that relates to feeling physical energy is when you first meet someone, you may instantly feel unsettled or scared. This is you feeling that person's energy. Although you intuitively don't feel right about the person, you know that you have to be polite and not judgemental so you may try to ignore that first initial intuitive warning. If you do go against your first gut reaction to the person and later become close to them, you may go on to find out that the person doesn't end up treating you well or that the they are dangerous.

Each of us are born with our own unique intuition that allows us to feel warning signs. It also gives us information about what is around us by using our 'sixth sense' to pick up things that our other five senses can't register. Our intuition enables us to pick up on energy around us.

Not all energy is negative, energy can be positive as well. When you space clear an area you want to remove the stagnant, negative energy and replace it with positive, new energy.

There are many different emotional and physical feelings and signs which highlight the need for you to space clear your environment, yourself and your home, they are:

ILLNESS

When someone has been ill or is ill in the home it can affect the emotions and energy of all of the people who live in or visit the home, as well as the energy of the space. It is very important that you take time to clear the space to get rid of any of the stagnant energy or remnants of feelings or emotions that are as a result of the illness.

Space clearing not only lifts the energy up in the home it also can help to uplift the people that are in and around the home, it can even help to motivate the person who is ill and give them a positive energy boost to help them to heal.

STRESS/DEPRESSION

Most people will experience stress or depression at some stage in their life, or have an important person in their life experience it. It is during these times, or after the stress or depression has occurred, that it is essential that you space clear your home so that you can recharge, de-stress and reenergize yourself and everyone else who lives in the home.

It can sometimes be helpful to have a positive reminder or a routine that gives you comfort in times of stress. When you space clear your home or room, or have a positive routine such as lighting candles, burning essential oils or incense, this can help you calm down and remember that you will be OK. Some people enjoy looking at the flame of the candle while others relax just by smelling the essential oils or incense. Other people may just need to feel like they are doing something different to switch their current thoughts or mindsets to something positive.

Everyone is unique and individual so it is up to you to find out what resonates the most. Try to think about the positive things you like to do to de-stress yourself or would like to do if you had a chance to.

ANGER/FIGHTING

Anger, aggression and fighting all carry powerful emotions and energy. Powerful emotions which are both positive and negative do leave an energy imprint in the area that they occur in. An example of negative energy or emotion is when you walk into an area and suddenly feel really angry or stressed when you were fine a few minutes earlier. If you have experienced this, you may be intuitively picking up on someone else's angry energy that is around you, or the area that you are standing in may have a lot of residual energy from past battles, fights or aggressive situations that have occurred there. If an area has a lot of residual negative energy you should not expect to go and space clear the whole area, but you do need to be mindful of how you are feeling— try to lift up and clear your energy before you return home.

Try to remove any negative or stressed energy from yourself by consciously remembering they are not your feelings, you are feeling someone else's emotions because you are happy, loved and enjoying yourself. Imagine that you are shining brightly inside and out with golden light, surround yourself in a bubble of gold light and feel all of the negativity disappearing.

It is important that you clear your own personal energy before returning to your home so that you don't bring any negativity with you. Keep your energy positive and bring that positive energy back into your home environment.

IF SOMEONE HAS PASSED AWAY

Besides love, grief is one of the strongest emotions a person can have. Grief can stick to people energetically, it is a very thick, heavy emotion that can have lasting effects on people physically and emotionally.

Grief doesn't only affect people physically and emotionally, sometimes when someone has passed away in a home there can be residual energy left behind from the deceased person. It doesn't necessarily have to be a negative energy, though, because the person may have passed very peacefully in their sleep or with all of their loved ones around them. It is just that the family members and friends who visit or enter the home have their own grief and emotions attached to that person and their belongings and they may feel this energy strongly around them when they are inside the home.

It can be very uplifting or helpful for family members if someone comes in and helps them to space clear the area or smudge the area to clear and lift the energy up. By space clearing the home the family and friends will not feel so heavy or upset when they enter the home.

If someone has passed in a traumatic, violent or unexpected way in a home it is very important that the home is 'smudged' (the buring of herbs—see page 42) and space cleared to get rid of any of the trapped energy that may be stored there.

It is also important to space clear the energy in a home if you are selling the home or moving into a place that you know someone passed away in.

SCARED/UNEASY/NIGHTMARES

Having broken sleep due to nightmares, restlessness or being scared is not good for anyone. It is very important that we as humans get as much sleep and rest as we can so that our bodies and energy can regenerate.

Sometimes we may have nightmares due to things that have happened to us in the past, or it could be something that we have seen or heard during the day. If someone has been watching horror or thriller movies or read books about these things it can make them feel unsettled or scared before they go to sleep.

Another unsettling thing can be staying in a home by yourself when you are not used to it, you may be used to having other people around you or be used to living in a different area. By space clearing you can remove any unsettled or scared energy, this can help you to sleep better at night and relax.

Divorce/Relationship Break-Ups

Relationship break-ups are incredibly painful and hard on all of the people concerned, often people will leave a home or will spend time away from the home environment due to the relationship break-up. It is essential during this unsettling time that you space clear your home and smudge yourself so that you can begin to move forward in your life and in your relationship area.

If there are any items, personal belongings or pieces of furniture that hold sad memories or past hurts for you it can be helpful if you donate these items to someone in need or try to clear the energy from these items if you do not want to donate them. Remember that every item holds energy from its owner, especially jewelry, clothing or anything that is held close to a person's body.

Robbery or Vandalism in the Home

People can feel like they have been violated after a personal robbery, home invasion or vandalism of their home. All sense of security and privacy can feel like it has been lost and there can be a fear that this kind of act might happen again.

When someone else's energy has entered your home without your permission, or has intruded on your own personal space, it is very important that you claim your space back. You can claim your space back by space clearing and reaffirming to yourself that you are safe and protected. Also affirm that this is your space and no one must enter it without your permission.

It can also be helpful to put some extra protection up and around your home that you can visually see so that it reaffirms to you that you are OK and you are protected. There are various talismans and protection symbols that you can use and deities, gods and goddesses that you can call upon for help.

Signs Around The Home

STAGNANT ENERGY

Energy in homes can become blocked or stagnant and this can happen even if a stressful event hasn't occurred. Just as we should clean our homes to get rid of any dust, dirt or rubbish we must also clean and clear the energy. Even though you can't see the stagnant energy you will be able to feel it. This stagnant energy can feel like a heavy energy which makes you feel tired, depressed or unmotivated. Each room can hold pockets of stagnant energy which need to be cleared so that the positive new energy can come in.

Often you may not notice at first that your home feels stagnant, because you are always there you become used to the energy, it isn't until you visit someone else's home or go on a holiday and stay somewhere else that you realize how different the energy is. How often have you gone on a holiday and thought, wow this hotel or this place feels so amazing? You then return home and feel like you are walking back into the same old, heavy energy that you left behind when you left. This is a big indicator that it is time to space clear your home.

MOVING INTO A NEW HOME

It is very exciting to move into a new home, it is a time of new beginnings and possibilities and with those new beginnings comes positive energy. Before you move into your new home it is essential that you space clear the place to get rid of any residual energy from the previous home owners or tenants, the area itself and any other energy that has attached itself to the space.

HOUSE NEEDING TO BE SOLD

If you have had your home on the market for sale for quite some time and it hasn't sold there may be a reason for this, the energy in your home may need to be cleared. Try to think what has gone on in the home, have there been any relationship break-ups, illness, death or depression? If you have said yes to any of these things you will definitely have to clear that residual energy out. Even if you can't feel the stagnant or negative energy the potential buyers looking at your home for the first time will feel it.

It is also important to make sure that all owners of the house are ready to sell the home and are equally willing to move. If one of the owners doesn't want to sell it can block the energy or make it harder to sell.

ELECTRICAL ITEMS PLAYING UP

In some homes there are constant electrical problems with lights going on and off, light bulbs blowing continuously, televisions and computers burning out and not working. These electrical problems can seem normal to some people, and they can be straightforward, but what if you have had an electrician check your wiring to see what is going on and they can't find any problems at all? This is when you know it is not an electrical problem with the home, it is an energy problem.

It is important to realize that spirits are made up of energy and they can manipulate this energy to make things happen to electrical items—this doesn't have to be a scary or negative thing, it can sometimes be their way of getting your attention to let you know that they are with you. Sometimes, your passed loved ones might play with the electrical items to get your attention.

It can be annoying and expensive to have to deal with this so it is a good idea to space clear the home to make sure that you get rid of these lower or negative energies that may be causing mischief in your home. But please note that space clearing won't remove any positive energies or your passed loved ones.

CHAPTER 2

TYPES OF ENERGY IN THE HOME

There are many different types of energy that can be found in your home; you will have your own energy there as well as the energy of other people that live with you, including your pets. There are also other energies that can be present in the home that you may not consciously be aware of, some of these energies are positive and are there to help you, and some of the energies can be negative or a bit mischievous.

It is important that you realize that you are the boss in your own home, you do not need to put up with any energy that you do not want there. As we go through some of the different types of energy that you may encounter in your home, it is up to you to decide if you feel like it applies to your home or not, and if you want to space clear and get rid of certain energies or not.

As mentioned earlier please note that you will not be clearing out any positive energies such as your passed loved ones, spirit guides or angels if you space clear or smudge, it will only clear out anything that should not be there or that is negative.

PASSED LOVED ONES

Your passed loved ones are always around you, not only when you are at home. They are guiding you, protecting you and trying to let you know that they are around you. Sometimes you will feel your passed loved ones physically, at other times you may receive signs from them or have different things that cannot be explained happen to you, around you and in your home.

An easy way for your passed loved ones to communicate with you or to give you a sign is through the electrical items in your home such as the lights, televisions, radios, ovens, alarm clocks, phones and door bells. Your passed loved ones may turn the electrical items off and on, make them not work, blow the fuse or even put a TV show or song on that you need to watch or listen to.

Please do not be afraid of any of the signs that your passed loved ones send to you, it is just their way to let you know that they are still around you and they still exist. You do not have to smudge to get rid of your passed loved ones, they will go if you ask them, to but if you don't want them to go they don't need to.

ORIGINAL LAND OR HOME OWNERS

In some homes there is a feeling of being watched or a feeling that you are trespassing on someone else's land, this can be you intuitively picking up on the original home owners or land owners of the home that you are living in.

Sometimes a passed spirit is so attached to their home or land that they keep coming back there to visit or they are stuck there by their emotional attachment to the place. They can also get caught up in what is going on with the current family that lives in their old home, the spirit can get confused and think that it is still their home and they can wonder who these people are who are living in their home.

Original passed land owners or home owners do not necessarily go out of their way to cause mischief for the current home owners, they just sometimes get in the way energetically by becoming too involved in the drama and activity within the home. Often you would see these passed spirits as a shadow, a quick glint of a bright orb of light or you may feel uneasy like you are being judged or watched by someone.

RESIDUAL ENERGY FROM EVENTS THAT HAVE OCCURRED

There can be residual energy from events that have occurred in a home, usually the residual energy is from traumatic events due to the strong nature of the emotions and energy that comes with trauma.

It can be quite unsettling going into a home that has had significant traumatic events happen there. People may feel tense, angry, frustrated or depressed for no particular reason, this is especially true for sensitive, empathetic people. You may not realize why you feel the way you do until you find out the history of the home or what events may have gone on there. This energy can be easily released and uplifted by space clearing and smudging.

SPIRIT GUIDES

Your Spirit Guides are very similar to your passed loved ones, they are here to help you and to protect you. You may feel your Spirit Guides physically in your home, or you may see them out of the corner of your eye as little orbs of white light flickering past.

It is not necessary to space clear to get rid of your Spirit Guides because they are positive spirits who are here to help you. They will not make you feel uneasy or scared, they are very loving and uplifting in their energy.

SPIRITS/GHOSTS—POSITIVE AND NEGATIVE

I don't like the term 'ghosts', I prefer to use the word 'spirits', but I do understand that there is a need to differentiate between the positive and negative spirits. Negative spirits can be called lower entities, ghosts or dark energies and they are the mischievous spirits that can make you feel uneasy in your home, and they can move items around, affect the electrical items and make people feel depressed, anxious and stressed.

Normal spirits who are positive spirits, are not your passed loved ones, friends or spirit guides, they are just spirits who are attracted to your home for some particular reason, or they could be spirits that are passing through that area at the time. These normal positive spirits do not try to scare you or harm you in any way they just are inquisitive and like to see what is going on in your home.

Traditional Indigenous land owners

The traditional indigenous land owners, passed and living, are culturally and spiritually connected to many pieces of land that homes are now built on. Some of the land that homes have been built on carries a lot of ancestral and cultural history with sometimes many hundreds of years' worth of rituals and beliefs embedded into that area. This happens in indigenous areas in countries all around the world.

It is very important that people research and try to find out as much as they can about who originally lived on the land that their home is built on. If you do find out that it has been traditional indigenous land it is a good idea to pay your respects to the traditional land owners' spirits by acknowledging them and asking them for permission for you and your loved ones to live there. You can easily do this by smudging the home and asking them in your mind, or out loud, for their permission. Try to let them know that you acknowledge that it is their land and you respect them and their culture.

There have been some cases that I have come across where people have not realized that their home has been built on traditional tribal lands. These people couldn't understand why there was so much going wrong in their home with their electrics, their plumbing and with their relationships and family life. It was because they had not asked for permission from the traditional indigenous spirits because they were unaware that they should do this. After finding this out and after honoring and respecting the traditional spirits they found that their electrical, plumbing and relationship problems all began to go away and they could feel happy and at ease in their home.

ENERGY ATTACHED TO ANTIQUE OR SECOND HAND OBJECTS

It is important that you be mindful of any second hand or antique object that you bring into your home because energy does attach itself to objects. Jewelry and spiritual or religious objects carry a lot of the previous owner's energy that is why you should smudge the items as soon as you bring them into your home. If you don't smudge the items you may pick up on the energy of the previous owners especially if you are quite intuitive and empathetic and you wear someone else's jewelry.

If you bring a piece of jewelry or an item into your home that was previously owned by someone you love that is completely fine because you are bringing happy, loving energy into your home and it is from a person that you know and love. This is a positive thing.

The Little Girl, The Dolls And The Old Friend

A good example of the types of energy that can be in a home occurred a few years ago when I was called out to space clear an expensive riverside mansion. The owners had contacted me because they were having a lot of problems with their new home that had been built right on a beautiful river.

I went to visit the home to see what I could sense and to see if I could help the family out, when I entered the home I was blown away at how opulent it was, it was brand new and spread out over three luxurious levels with a lift operating between each level. I was surprised that such a new home could have so many problems.

The owners were a married couple with two little girls and they were very upset because there had been no end of trouble with this new dream home of theirs. There were constant electrical problems with lights going on and off, security systems being activated. The owners had electricians and various tradesmen investigate what was going on in the home. None of them could work out what the problem was and it was costing the owners a lot of money and heartache.

Another problem the family was having was that their youngest daughter had been having terrible nightmares since they moved into the home and she was terrified to sleep in her beautiful new bedroom. This bedroom was fit for a princess, it was decked out with all of the mod cons and beautiful furniture, but she was not happy in it.

I decided to inspect the house to see what I could see and sense, as I was walking around the kitchen and the lounge room I noticed a happy male spirit sitting in the main lounge area. I mentioned this man to the male owner and he asked me to ask who he was and to find out what he wanted. The male spirit went on to tell me his name and explained about his love of boats and that he was a friend of the male owner. As I was telling the owners this their faces changed and a look of recognition came over their faces. They realized this was their friend who had just recently passed away from a heartattack weeks before they moved into their new home.

After talking to the owners and the male spirit more I realized that he was the one that was accidently causing the electrical problems, he didn't mean to hurt them or harm them he was just trying to connect with them and let them know he was still around them. After I told them this they calmed down a lot. The male spirit was happy that they acknowledged him and he said he wouldn't try to get their attention in that way anymore. I knew that this would fix their electrical problems and I also knew that I didn't need to smudge or remove their friend's energy because he was a good spirit, he just wanted to be heard.

I left the lounge room and walked around the home, the owner's youngest daughter took me to her bedroom. When I walked into the bedroom the first thing I noticed was the antique display cabinet full of old dolls, it was situated in the far corner of the little girl's bedroom. In that corner there was a lot of dark energy, no light shined there and it felt very cold.

As I walked around the bedroom I noticed the little girl didn't want to go near the antique cabinet and dolls. I asked her what she felt about the dolls and she said to me that they scared her, she could see them move at night and it was terrifying for her. She often asked her mother to cover the cabinet up but her mother didn't understand what was going on.

I asked the little girl to go and play downstairs while I spoke to her parents. After she left I asked the parents where they got the antique cabinet and dolls from and they said

21

that they had purchased them from an antique store because they thought it would look good in their daughter's room.

I explained to them that antiques actually carry residual energy from the previous owners and that it is important to clear the energy of the items. I also let them know what I felt about the darkness in that corner and that I felt that there was some negative and dark energy attached to the dolls in the cabinet. I said to them if they didn't want to get rid of the dolls they needed to at least space clear the room and put the dolls away out of their daughter's room so that she could feel happy in her room and begin to sleep again at night.

The owners agreed with what I suggested and I used a sage smudge stick in the little girl's room. I smudged each corner of her room and asked for all negativity to be removed, I also smudged the whole house in every corner doing the same thing. After smudging the home I asked the owners to open up some of the windows to let the energy out. I also left a smudge stick with them and taught them how to smudge if ever they felt like they needed to.

A few days later I contacted the owners to see how they were going in their house and how their little girl was sleeping. They let me know that they were very happy that everything seemed to have calmed down electrically in the home and their little girl was no longer scared of sleeping in her room since they packed up the antique dolls and put them down in the basement.

CHAPTER 3

TOOLS AND TECHNIQUES TO SPACE CLEAR

Crystals

CRYSTALS USED IN SPACE CLEARING

Crystals are wonderful natural healers from the mineral kingdom—they are full of positive energy and they can help you to clear the energy of a space instantly. Each crystal has its own unique healing property and energy, you can use a crystal by itself, hang a crystal from a window or ceiling or choose to put multiple crystals together that resonate with you. You may even like to wear a crystal as a talisman or have a crystal in your pocket, there are so many different ways to harness the positive energy of crystals.

CLEANSING YOUR CRYSTALS

It is important that you cleanse your crystals when you first bring them into your home. This is important so that you can remove any old energies or memories which may have been stored inside the crystal.

To cleanse your crystal you can use any of the following methods:

△ *Leave the crystals out in the direct sunlight for a day or longer*

△ *Put the crystals out in the full moon*

△ *Place the crystals into the earth, with their point facing up for approx. 2 to 3 days*

△ *Use incense or smudge sticks and wave the smoke over all sides of the crystal*

△ *Put the crystal in sea water or rock salt water*

△ *Place the crystal on the sand at the beach*

△ *Visualize and put good intent into the crystal asking for all negative energy to be removed*

Once you have cleansed your crystals you then can begin to place them around your home to help lift the energy and keep the home a positive space where people enjoy spending time.

USING CRYSTALS TO UPLIFT AND REMOVE NEGATIVE/STAGNANT ENERGY IN A HOME

Place crystal clusters such as amethyst or citrine in and around your home, you may even like to have bowls of crystals on your window sills, on top of a fireplace, bookcase or even have a crystal cluster or bowl of crystals in the middle of your dining room table.

The following crystals work very well together and are

great for clearing energy in your home.

Amethyst
Color: Purple

Healing Properties: Helps to calm and protect you. Removes negativity and helps to overcome fears and reoccurring nightmares. It enhances spiritual awareness.

An amethyst gets rid of anger, anxiety and helps to balance out emotions of loss and grief.

Place an amethyst crystal under your pillow or next to your bed to get rid of nightmares and help you to sleep.

An amethyst cluster (a crystal made up with many smaller crystals) can be placed in any room of your home to clear unwanted energies and to calm the house down. You can also place amethyst on top of your air conditioners, microwaves and television sets to reduce the radiation in your home.

Aventurine
Color: Green
(also comes in brown, red, blue and peach)

Healing Properties: Aventurine is a great crystal for courage; it also helps you to feel happy and positive. This crystal will help you feel creative, confident and strong. It will help your heart and lungs.

Place an aventurine in your pocket when you are starting a new job, business or class and it will give you a confidence boost. Place a piece of aventurine by itself or with other crystals in the living room/family room and kitchen.

Black Obsidian
Color: Black

Healing Properties: Black Obsidian is a very powerful crystal that can help to disperse any negative energy that is around you personally or that is in your home. This crystal calms the energy down in a home and helps to keep the place free of negativity.

You can place a piece of black obsidian by the front and back door of your home to provide extra protection or you can place it in your bedroom to help you to feel safe, secure and calm. If you feel frightened or nervous hold a piece of black obsidian in the palm of your hand.

Black Tourmaline
Color: Black

Healing Properties: Black tourmaline is very similar in its healing properties to black obsidian. It is a crystal that gets rid of negative energies so that positive energy, wellbeing and prosperity can come in. By getting rid of the negative energies black tourmaline improves the energy and vibration of the air where it is located.

You may like to wear a piece of black tourmaline in jewelry or carry a piece in your pocket. In the home it is a good idea to keep black tourmaline in the bedroom next to your bed or under your pillow because this will help you to sleep better and wake more refreshed, it will also space clear and protect the room that you sleep in. For extra protection you may even like to put or hang a piece of black tourmaline at the front and back door of your home.

Carnelian
Color: Orange
(also comes in red, pink and brown)
Healing Properties: Carnelian is a great crystal for feeling confident and for helping you feel secure in your life.

This crystal helps you to trust in yourself and your gifts and helps you to overcome fears. It also calms anger down.

Place a carnelian in your pocket or in a crystal pouch to help calm you, or have a piece of carnelian in your office or bedroom to give you a boost of confidence and positivity.

Citrine
Color: Bright Yellow and Orange
Healing Properties: This is a crystal which holds no negativity, it is one of the only crystals that you do not need to cleanse. It brings positivity and abundance into your home and your life.

Place a piece of citrine or a citrine cluster in the back left hand corner of your home to increase your wealth because this is your wealth corner according to Feng Shui. Citrine is known as the wealth stone.

Clear Quartz
Color: Clear
Healing Properties: Clear quartz is a fantastic general all-purpose healing crystal, it helps with concentration and removes negativity.

Clear quartz helps your immune system, it brings balance to your body and helps you to think more clearly. It also helps enhance psychic abilities and meditation.

Hematite
Color: Silver/Metallic Gray

Healing Properties: Hematite is a very grounding and protective crystal, it makes us feel safe and secure and rebalances us. It is the stone of the mind so it can help you to concentrate, think and focus on what you need to do.

Hematite can also prevent you from absorbing any negative energy from other people or places, which is why it is an important and powerful crystal to have in your home environment. You can place this crystal anywhere in your home. Hematite is also great if you have migraines or headaches you just need to place a piece of hematite on your forehead or behind your ears, you will feel your headache go away.

Red Jasper
Color: Red/Maroon

Healing Properties: Red Jasper is a protective crystal, it helps to ground your energy and guard you against physical threats. It is also a great crystal to stimulate passion in your personal and work life and it helps you to get creative, to manifest new ideas and move forward toward new beginnings in your life.

You can wear red jasper in a pendant, bracelet or keep a piece in your pocket, or you may like to place a piece of red jasper in your home near your front door or in your office or study area to absorb any negativity and radiation. You can also keep red jasper in your car to prevent road rage, theft or car accidents.

Rose Quartz
Color: Pink

Healing Properties: Rose quartz is a very loving soothing crystal which helps heal broken hearts and hurt feelings. It calms and gets rid of fears, anxiety and hyperactivity.

This crystal helps you to build self-confidence, self-trust and encourages love, compassion and understanding.

Wear a rose quartz pendant over your heart to feel loved and confident. Place a rose quartz crystal next to your bed to help you calm down before sleep.

To help your relationship place a rose quartz next to your bed or place a piece in the room in the back right corner of your home because this will boost your love and relationships according to Feng Shui.

Smokey Quartz
Color: Gray, Brown and Black

Healing Properties: Smokey quartz is an excellent crystal for relieving stress, fear or any other negative emotions. Smokey quartz transforms the dense negative energy into positive energy it is a very helpful stone to have in the home because it is very calming and it encourages inner strength and serenity.

Place a piece of smokey quartz in your kitchen and/or living room to help keep the energy uplifted, or place it in your home office or workplace to enhance organizational skills.

Tiger Eye
Color: Gold and Brown
Healing Properties: Tiger eye is fantastic to help you ground your energy and feel more stable in your life. It helps you to organize yourself and feel confident in times of change.

This crystal helps you to feel secure in your surroundings and calms anger down. It also helps you to become more creative and focused, so it is great for new beginnings in the home, new business ideas or jobs.

FENG SHUI PLACEMENT OF CRYSTALS IN YOUR HOME

According to the ancient art of Feng Shui if you place particular crystals in strategic places around your home it can have positive effects on all aspects of your and your family's life.

Please see the diagram to find out about each area of the home and how it relates to different parts of your life. There are also examples of which crystals to use in each separate place in your home.

You may choose to place a crystal in one area that you want to focus on or you may like to put a crystal in each area, it is totally up to you what you decide to do. Remember, you must cleanse your crystals first before you use them.

Feng Shui Home Bagua Chart

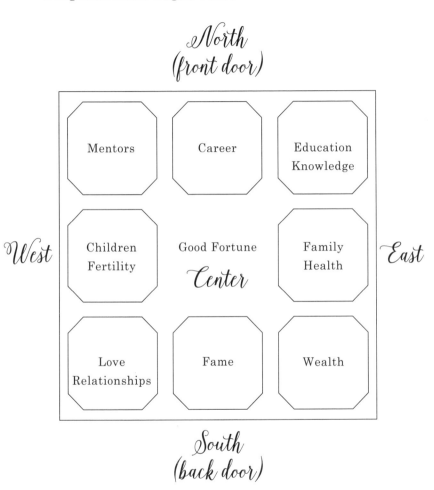

Crystals to use in each area of the home

Northwest = Mentor Corner (Color: Purple/Gray)

Place an amethyst cluster or crystal in the northwest corner of your home to encourage positive support from mentors, helpful people and the Universe.

North = Career Area (Color: Dark Blue/Black)

Place a sodalite or lapis lazuli crystal in the northern area of your home to enhance your intuition and to help you to make the right career decisions.

Northeast = Education and Knowledge Corner (Color: Blue/Green)

Place a piece of turquoise in the northeast corner of your home for balance, positive energy, wisdom, self-knowledge and wonderful educational opportunities.

Southwest = Love and Relationships Corner (Color: Pink/Skin Earth Tones)

Place a large piece of rose quartz cluster in the southwest corner of your home to encourage or attract a wonderful long lasting, equal loving relationship.

South = Fame Area (Color: Red)

Place or hang a large red jasper crystal in the southern area of your home to enhance your recognition and fame and to improve your career prospects.

Southeast = Wealth Corner (Color: Purple/Green/Gold)

Place a cluster of citrine in the southeast corner of your home to bring wealth and prosperity to you and those in your family.

East = Family and Health (Color: Purple/Green/Gold)

Place a jade crystal in the eastern area of your home to promote good health, long life, wealth and happiness for you and your family.

West = Children and Fertility (Color: White/Pastel Colors)

Place a piece of rainbow moonstone in the western area of your home to increase your fertility and to also bring positive energy to any children in your home.

Center of Home = Good Fortune (Color: Yellow/ Earth Tones)

Place a piece of citrine in the center of your home to increase the abundance and good fortune in your life. Citrine's positive energy will uplift all members of your household.

You can place a single crystal in each of the areas above because all of the crystals are excellent space clearers, however you don't need to just wear the crystals as a talisman or place them individually around your home, you can place your crystals in specific geometric patterns which are called crystal grids. People use crystal grids to clear the space in their home or to bring a specific intention or energy into their home. When you use a crystal grid and add your energy and intentions, it can often be more powerful than using a single crystal for an intended goal.

CRYSTAL GRIDDING

What is Crystal Gridding?

Crystals are great for space clearing an area, they can be used to change and enhance the vibrations of a home or office or even outdoor areas such as gardens, pool areas or ley lines.

To create a crystal grid you need to place specific crystals in strategic positions and locations within the space where you want to enhance or amplify the energy. Crystals are natural energy amplifiers, they are fantastic at creating positive uplifting energy in a space. To make a crystal grid you need to have more than one crystal because each crystal needs to link together in a network, you can use as many crystals as you want, there is no limit.

There are many different patterns that you can create when you make a crystal grid, usually the patterns are in a geometric pattern with one crystal in the center of the grid being the master crystal. Each grid has its own special purpose and is unique so you do not have to follow any strict rules to what you do with your crystal grid, there is no right or wrong way to create a crystal grid, the most important thing to do is to have the right intention when you make the grid and to also use crystals that have been cleansed.

How do you create a crystal grid?

It isn't hard to create a crystal grid, you can create a simple one that protects your home by using five crystals of your choice, I like to use black onyx, black obsidian or amethyst for this kind of grid because of their protective energy. I also like to use crystals that have one natural point on the end if they are available. If you don't have natural points it is ok to use tumbled crystals.

Tumbled crystals are natural crystals which have been polished or machine tumbled to make the surface of the crystal smooth to touch, it also gives the crystal a nice polished shine. Tumbled crystals are easy to hold in your hand and are not rough like natural crystals which may have sharp or rough edges or surfaces. Many people prefer to use tumbled crystals because they can wear them against their body without the edges scratching them. They are also sometimes referred to as tumbled stones.

Once you decide on the crystals that you want to use, you have to decide on the intent that you want to put into your crystal grid i.e. what is it that you want this crystal grid to achieve for you?

A Simple Five Crystal Pyramid Protection Grid for the Home

After you have decided on your intent, begin to place one crystal in each corner of your home or room that you want to protect. Leave one crystal to be the master crystal or center crystal in the middle of your home (or as close as possible to the middle) or room. For the master/center crystal I usually like to use a clear quartz because they are fantastic amplifiers.

The master crystal is responsible for communicating with

the other four crystals to help keep the energy going in harmony. You can also do this crystal grid with just four crystals, with one in each corner, but it is not as powerful as using the five crystals. When you use the five crystals you are harnessing the energy of the fifth crystal and by placing it in the center of the home or room it creates an amazing pyramid shape which is very powerful.

Here is an example of intention that you can say when you lay your protection grid down in your home. (Please note that you can add your own religious, spiritual or beliefs to this and create your own unique prayer or mantra that will serve you best.)

Prayer/Mantra/Intention for Protection of Family and Home

Please... *(direct this to whom you wish)* bless and protect this person/family that stands before you *(say all the names of your family and your animals here)* and all the people and animals who will come to live here in the future with my/our blessing. Please bring good health, abundance, happiness and love to this home.

Please... clear and cleanse this house of any negativity or stagnant energy that resides here and use my intention and these crystals to do this. Free this house of any and all that would do harm to any of us and protect us from any outsiders that would do us harm of any kind, for the good of all and harm to none.

We honor the traditional owners of this land both past and present with respect and thank them for having us on their land.

Thank you... we are grateful for everything that you help us with and provide us with each and every day.

Five Crystal Pyramid Protection Grid for the Home

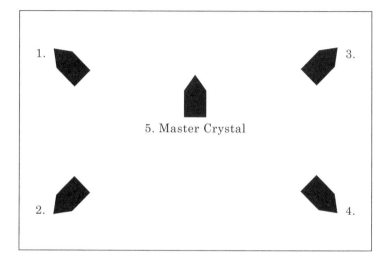

1.

3.

5. Master Crystal

2.

4.

Protection Grid for the Property including the Outside Areas

You can also make and use this crystal grid on a larger scale by placing one crystal in each corner outside of your home in your yard. Bury a crystal in each corner of your yard, state your intention and place the master crystal inside in the middle of your home. This will create an even larger protective energy for your home environment.

Prayer/Mantra/Intention for Protection of the complete Property/Home

Please... bless, clear, protect and cleanse this land of any negativity that resides here and use my intention and these crystals to do this. Please free this land of any negativity, stagnant energy and all that would do harm to any of us. Protect us from any outsiders that would do us harm of any kind, for the good of all and harm to none.

We honor the traditional owners of this land both past and present with respect and thank them for having us on their land.

Thank you... we are grateful for everything that you help us with and provide us with each and every day.

Protection Grid for the Property including the Outside Areas

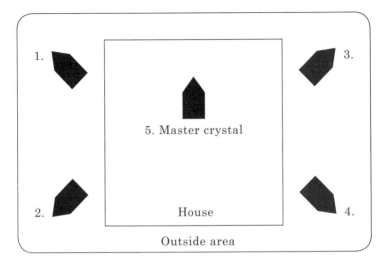

CRYSTAL GRIDDING ON A SMALLER SCALE

Crystal grids work on a smaller scale as well, you do not need to create a grid that covers your whole home, you may like to create a smaller grid with a specific intent that you can have in your bedroom, living room or office. You can place your crystal grid on a table, up on top of a bookshelf or even on top of a bedroom chest of drawers, it doesn't really matter where you place it as long as you know it is safe and out of the reach of young children.

You can leave your crystal grid in place for as long as you want or need it, but you should try to cleanse the crystals on a regular basis or when you feel like you need to.

Here is a suggestion of an abundance and prosperity grid that you may like to use in your home.

Abundance and Prosperity Grid
For this abundance and prosperity grid focus on what you would like to achieve and how you would like to have abundance and prosperity enter your life. Select the crystals that you would like to use or that resonate with you the most. I personally would use a big citrine cluster or piece of citrine, a large piece of aventurine as well as some clear quartz points, some jade, red jasper and any other crystals that you feel drawn to.

The best place to put this abundance and prosperity grid is in the back left hand corner of your home in your wealth corner or next to your computer, in your office or wherever you spend a lot of time working at home.

You can make this grid in any way that you feel drawn to, please see this example of how I would usually make my abundance and prosperity crystal grid:

Abundance and Prosperity Grid

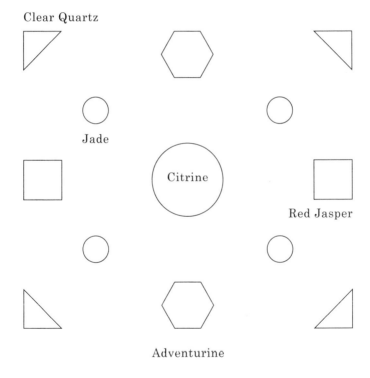

Clear Quartz

Jade

Citrine

Red Jasper

Adventurine

Intent

Just remember the most important thing about crystal gridding and space clearing is the intent that you put behind it, make sure you are clear about what your intent is and stick to it.

Smudging And Smudge Sticks

Smudging

Smudging is an ancient ritual which involves burning specific herbs to clear out and get rid of any negative energies or entities. The burning herbs create a protective smoke around a person, object or a place. The traditional herbs used in Native American smudging ceremonies are cedar, sweet grass and sage. The herbs can be bound together with thread or string to form a smudge stick, or they can be placed in an abalone shell, which needs to have sand or soil in it to prevent it from overheating, you can also use a heat resistant bowl.

The word smudging traditionally comes from the Native American culture however there are many different cultures around the world who have their own type of ritual or smudging ceremony. Indigenous Australians are an example of this because they have their own form of smudging ceremony called a smoking ceremony. In the smoking ceremony various native plants such as eucalyptus leaves are burnt on top of a large piece of bark from a tree.

It is not only indigenous cultures that use smoke or smudging to clear out negative energies, many different religions have their own ceremonies to purify and protect a person or place. For example, during religious ceremonies in the Catholic Church the priest will use incense and frankincense to clear the energy and protect the church and all who are in it.

Smudging ceremonies focus on bringing balance to all aspects of a person: physically, spiritually and mentally, they are also used to create balance in the home and its environment.

The intent behind smudging is just as important as the actual smudging herbs. It is very important that you smudge when you are ready to clear out any old, negative or stale energy in and around your home. Smudging is also a great self-care activity to keep your energy positive, uplifted and recharged.

HOW TO SMUDGE YOUR HOME

The first thing that you should do before you begin to smudge your home is to have a clear intent about what you want to achieve by smudging. Most people have a similar intent for their home—they would like it and all of the people in it to be safe, protected and healthy, and for all that visit or live there to feel uplifted, happy and relaxed when inside. You may have a different intent, just make sure you are clear.

Equipment needed to Smudge your Home
You have to have the right equipment to smudge your home, you can use variations on the below, but for a traditional Native American smudging ceremony this is what you will need:

△ *Herbs such as sage, cedar or sweet grass either in loose leaf form or tied into a smudge stick*
△ *Sage is used to get rid of negative energy and to keep negative energy out*
△ *Cedar is used to purify a space*
△ *Sweet Grass is used to bring in good energy*
△ *Matches or a lighter*
△ *An abalone or paua shell, or a heat resistant bowl*
△ *Dirt or sand to put in the shell or bowl*
△ *A large feather or feather prayer fan (this is optional, you can also use your hand)*

Once you have all of these things you are ready to begin to smudge yourself and your home. Try to make sure that you will not be disturbed during the smudging process because you will need to focus on your intent.

Step One: Place a small amount of sand or dirt in the shell or bowl, then place your loose herbs on top and light them with the matches or a lighter and gently blow on them.

If you have a smudge stick you do not need to use the bowl or shell however you can use it to catch any of the herbs which fall off. Light the smudge stick with matches or a lighter and gently blow on it to get it smoking. If the fire goes out just relight it as needed.

Step Two: Start smudging in the most northern part of your home, walk with the lit herbs in the smoking shell or smudge stick in a clockwise direction, starting from the north. Fan the smoke with your feather or hand and think of your intent or state it out loud, ask for all negativity to be removed. Make sure that you fan the smoke into all corners of every room in the home, even behind doors.

Step Three: After you've walked around the whole house in a clockwise direction you should end up back at your original starting point. Once you have smudged your home you can smudge yourself by fanning the smoke over your face and body with the feather, or your hand, to purify yourself.

Step Four: When you have finished with the smudging herbs it is important to snuff the smudge stick or loose herbs out in the sand or dirt. If possible, bury the old sand or dirt with the loose herbs in it outside under a tree. If you can't do this just dispose of it thoughtfully

Note: Smudge sticks can be used more than once depending on their size.

Step Five: After smudging your home and yourself it is

important that you open up all of the curtains and windows in your home (if possible) to let all of the old negative energy out.

Please note that it is important that you do not smudge in small enclosed areas if you are are asthmatic, pregnant or have babies or small children around you. If any of these things apply to you, you may like to use an incense stick or an aromatherapy spritzer spray instead, they are just as powerful as it is the intent that accompanies them that really makes a difference.

INCENSE

Incense has been used in its basic form since the beginning of human history to clear energy and change the emotions of the people who are around it. Our ancestors realized that some herbs, plants and spices emit distinctive and sometimes very potent scents when burnt.

Most cultures throughout history have used sacred herbs, plants and spices for their rituals, ceremonies and specific healing purposes. The scents that are produced by the various herbs, plants and spices would help to clear, disinfect and purify the energy around the home and environment as well as change the mood of the people and heighten their senses.

You can still use incense today to clear out any negativity, cleanse your home and to relax your mind and body. There are many different types of incense available to purchase, try different varieties and if you find one that suits you and you enjoy its scent you can regularly use it to clear the energy in and around your home.

The following list highlights what each incense is and what it is used for. Please note that there are many different types of incense around and many different belief systems connected to them.

INCENSE	USAGE
Bamboo	Luck and Protection
Cedar	Purification, Protection and Release
Champa	Harmony, Clearing and Protection
Desert Sage	Purification, Wisdom and Protection
Eucalyptus Leaf	Healing and Protection
Frankincense	Purification and Spiritual Growth
Jasmine Flowers	Relaxation and Sleep
Lavender	Clear and Cleanse
Lilac	Peace, Harmony and Protection
Nag Champa	Cleanse and Clear
Pine Needles/Cones	Protection and Health
Rose Petals	Love, Success and Protection
Rosemary	Concentration and Memory
Sage	Protection and Clearing
Sweet Grass	Purification and Clearing

How to Space Clear with Incense

To space clear or smudge your home with incense you need to use a similar procedure to the smudging ceremony.

Step One: Decide on your intent and choose which incense you would like to use. Try to use incense that you like the smell of otherwise it can be counterproductive if you are trying to clear out negativity and you don't feel positive about the smell.

Step Two: Start by lighting the incense in the most northern part of your home, walk with the lit incense in a clockwise direction, starting from north. Fan the smoke from the incense with your hand and think of your intent, or state it out loud, and ask for all negativity to be removed. Make sure that you fan the smoke into all corners of every room in the home, even behind doors.

Step Three: After walking around the whole house in a clockwise direction you should end up back at your original starting point. Once you have cleared the energy in your home you can clear and purify the energy around yourself by fanning the incense smoke over your face and body with your hand.

Step Four: When you have finished with the incense stick it is important to snuff it out or let it continue to burn in an incense holder.

Step Five: After space clearing your home and yourself with incense it is important that you open up all of the curtain and windows in your home (if possible) to let all of the old negative energy out.

ESSENTIAL OILS

Essential oils are great for people to use in their home environment if they do not want to use smudge sticks, incense or herbs due to the smells and smoke that they create. Essential oils are also great for keeping the energy positive around the home and they smell fantastic.

How to Use Essential Oils to Clear the Energy in your Home

There are various different ways that you can use essential oils to space clear your home, you can use an oil burner, a diffuser or a spritzer/spray bottle that you add distilled water to and spray around your home.

It is very important that you try to use only quality essential oils not the cheaper aromatherapy or fragrance oils for the best possible space clearing energy. The reason that I suggest using essential oils is because essential oils contain therapeutic benefits whereas fragrance oils smell nice but do not contain the same healing properties as essential oils.

Here is a list of essential oils that can be used in your home for space clearing.

Please note that some essential oils are not appropriate for use during pregnancy, or if you have epilepsy or certain allergies and sensitivities. Research or ask your doctor or naturopath about the essential oils you are using if you have any of these conditions.

ESSENTIAL OIL	USAGE
Bergamot	Balancing and Uplifting
Frankincense	Mental Strength, Peace, Purification
Geranium	Release, Calm and Clarity
Jasmine	Self Confidence and Optimism
Lavender	Cleansing, Detoxifying and Balance
Myrrh	Clarity, Focus and Strength
Peppermint	Cleansing and Detoxifying
Rose	Love and Peace

SEA SALT

Using natural sea salt is a very powerful, safe and effective way to space clear and lift the energy in your home environment. You can buy ready-made sea salt or you can make your own by evaporating seawater so that only the salt remains. I prefer using natural sea salt instead of using normal household processed table salt.

How to Use Sea Salt to Space Clear your Home
To cleanse and space clear a home with sea salt you should place small amounts of sea salt in bowls and put them in the four corners of your home, or four corners of the room that you wish to space clear. When you are placing the bowls down it is important that you state your intention that you wish to clear out any negativity energy from the space. It is up to you how long you want to leave the salt bowls out, but I would usually leave them for one to two days. When you are finished with the salt in the bowls try to bury the salt in the ground outside or throw it immediately into a bag and place it into a bin, do not reuse the salt because it will contain all the impurities and negativity energy.

If you don't want to leave sea salt out in bowls you can easily make a sea salt spritzer that you can spray in and around the home. To make your own sea salt spritzer dissolve two teaspoons of sea salt into some clean warm water and pour it into a spray bottle, you can use this whenever you need to.

CANDLES

Candles are an everyday item that many people have in their home, they may have decorative candles, emergency candles for use in the case of power outages, birthday cake candles or scented candles. It doesn't matter what type of candle it is, each has a specific purpose and that purpose is to bring light into an area, to get rid of darkness.

Candles can also be used for space clearing and to set positive intentions into a space. Setting an intention or making a wish is just like when you were a young child and you would make a wish before you blew out your birthday candles. Now as an adult you can make a wish or set an intention in your home. You may choose to light the candle because it smells nice and it relaxes you or you may like to light the candle and set an intention.

There are many different types of candles that you can use, it is personal preference which you choose. I am not too concerned by the size or shape of the candles that I use because I feel it is more important to focus on your intention and what you want to achieve by lighting the candle.

Just as there are many different kinds of candles, there are also many different colors of candles that you can use. It is important to know that each color does represent a different healing property and energy. Try to decide what it is that you want achieve by lighting the candle i.e. what is your intention—once you decide on your intention you can choose a candle in the color that matches that intention.

When you have an intention and match that intention to a

specific color which has those healing properties or energies, you increase the power and energy behind your intention.

You can even take it a step further and try to get a candle that has essential oils added to it so you can have the color of the candle that you want, the essential oil that you need and then all you need to do is add your intention to it.

Here is a list of colors that I relate to specific healing properties and energies, you may have your own ideas about which colors relate to different things so always go by what feels right for you, this is just a guide.

COLOR	HEALING PROPERTIES OR ENERGY
Yellow	Positivity, Abundance, Creativity
Red	Affection, Love, Passion
Pink	Compassion, Love, Relationships
Light Blue	Peace, Relaxation, Harmony
Dark Blue	Protection, Intuition
Green	Healing, Clearing, Good Fortune
Purple	Protection, Spiritual Connections
White	Purity, Clarity, Peace

How to Use your Candle to Space Clear Your Home

Once you have decided on your intention and you have the candle of your choice it is quite easy to set your intention with the use of a candle.

The first thing you need to do is make sure that the candle is safely in a small glass bowl, a candle holder or on a dish so that you don't burn yourself. When you are ready it is important that you focus on your intention, for example you may ask in your mind that you and everyone that resides in your home be safe, healthy and protected.

As soon as you feel you have your intention light your candle, I would then focus on walking from the northern part of your home and go into every room of your home, just as you would do if you were smudging your home with herbs or incense. Make sure that you have the candle lit throughout the whole process and that you are thinking of your intention or saying it out loud as you walk around.

Keep walking around the home in a clockwise direction until you end up back where you started. It is important that you do not blow your candle out when you are finished, you may choose to leave the candle burning (with supervision of course) or you can safely snuff your candle out with the bottom of a tea cup or with a candle snuffer. The reason you should not blow the candle out is because it blows out the intentions and disperses all the strong energy that you have just created.

If you still have some of your candle left and it has not melted completely it is important that you do not use this candle again for any other purpose, it has its own special intention so it will not be able to be used again. It is best to keep these candles separate from any other candles that you may have in your home.

You may like to repeat this process whenever you feel that you need to pick the energy up in your home or if you would like to put an intention out for a specific healing energy you can focus on a specific room in your home. For example, if you were looking for a new relationship you could focus on a red or pink candle and have it lit in your bedroom and/or relationship area (see the Feng Shui Bagua Chart on page 31 for more details).

WORDS OF AFFIRMATIONS

Words are very powerful things, they can make or break you, which is why it is important to think before you speak. Just as people can be affected by what other people say around them, so can the energy of your home. Try to be mindful of what you say in your home, it is important that you infuse your home with loving, positive thoughts, energy and words.

Each time you use positive words of affirmations in your home you are lifting the energy in the space. People who come to visit your home may wonder why they feel so happy to be in your space and you may notice that they don't want to rush off or leave.

To remind yourself of positive affirmations or prayers you could write some down and attach them to your fridge with a magnet, hang inspirational sayings in frames on the wall or even note down sayings on a calendar in your bedroom. It doesn't matter if you have these up on your wall or not, it just matters that you are consciously trying to put positive thoughts in your home.

You may like to write your own positive affirmations or you can try and use some of these examples:

Δ *My home and all who live and visit here are safe, loved and protected*

Δ *Only positive energies are allowed into this home, all other energies will not enter*

Δ *I am blessed and so are all that enter my home*

Δ *I am thankful for my home and thankful for everyone and everything in it*

Δ *All of my family, friends and myself are happy and healthy, as is my home*

Δ *Abundance comes in all forms to myself, my family and my friends instantly for the good of all and harm to none*

CLEARING SPACE WITH SOUND: CLAPPING, BELLS, DRUMS AND SINGING BOWLS

People can be affected both emotionally and physically by sounds and even if the sound is not heard its vibrations can be felt. Some sounds are very healing such as music, chimes, singing bowls and drums. You can use sounds to not only uplift and heal yourself, but also to space clear your home environment. A great thing about using sound to space clear is that it is not messy, it doesn't make any smells and there is no risk of the smoke alarm going off.

When you space clear your home you can use many different types of sound. For example you may like to sing, clap your hands, use a musical instrument or even turn the radio on or play a CD. It doesn't matter what sound or instrument you use to make the sound, it is the intent behind making the sound that is the most important thing.

Everyone is individual so it is totally up to you what you use to space clear your home with, there are a various different tools or instruments you can use, you may choose to use just one or you may like to use a variety of different tools.

I have listed a few examples of the more common instruments and tools below, try and find which ones you are drawn to or what feels right for you.

Clapping

Clapping is a very easy and effective tool for dispersing negative or stagnant energy in a room or home. It is important that you use loud, purposeful clapping with a positive intention in your mind about how you would like to clear the space and only have positive energy remain.

How to Space Clear with Clapping

△ *Make sure you take a deep breath in, then breathe out, get your body relaxed. When you are ready set your intention in your mind or state it out loud, for example you may say "I remove all negativity from this space, only positive energy remains".*

△ *Begin by using small quick claps, listen to hear what the sound is like, does it sound like a dull clap or a crisp clap? As you start clapping work your way up from small fast claps to bigger louder claps.*

△ *To uplift the energy in the space it is a good idea to start clapping from the middle of the room out into each corner*

of the room. You will notice the difference in the sound
of the clapping, when a space is clear and full of positive
energy the sound will be clear and crisp not dull.

Δ *When you feel you are finished shake your hands around*
in front of you at least three times and imagine that you
are clean from head to toe and filled with clear, bright
white light.

Bells

Bells have been used by various different cultures and
religions for many hundreds of years for things such as:
religious practices, announcing important information and
space clearing. When you clear a space with bells the room
feels clean, uplifted and fresh. There are many different
types of bells that you can use.

There are Tibetan bells, Nepalese bells, small and large
Balinese bells—the small bells are used for smaller spaces
and you can use the large bells for larger homes and spaces—
plus many more.

It is important that you choose a bell that feels right for
you, take note how it feels in your hand, is it too heavy or
too light? Do you like the sound of the bell? Each bell has its
own unique sound. Try many different kinds of bells out and
see if you prefer a higher toned bell or a bell with a lower
tone. Some people even like to look further into the bell to
see how it was made, where it was made and who made it.

The reason it is so important to have a bell that sounds
right for you is because if you have bell that doesn't sound
right to you or is out of tune it will be counterproductive for
you when you are space clearing. The sound will not clear

out the negative energy, it will make you feel frustrated and could increase the negative energy, so be very careful about the bell that you select.

How to Space Clear with Bells

Start at the entrance to your home or in the room in which you would like to space clear, focus on what your intention is. Walk clockwise around your home or room ringing the bell in each corner.

When you have rung the bell in each corner of the room, stand in the center of the room and ring your bell one or two more times. Listen to the sound of the bell, notice how differently it sounds once you have cleared the room. You will know that the room or your home has been successfully space cleared by the sound of the bell because it will resonate a lot more clearly and will have a wonderful uplifting feel to it.

Open your windows up after you have cleared your home so that all of the old energy can leave.

Singing Bowls

In the same way that clapping or using bells can clear energy in your home, using a singing bowl can also help you to space clear your home. A singing bowl is a wonderful tool to create positive energy in your home environment, it is great if you use it regularly because the more you use it and get used to using it the more powerful the bowl becomes and the better it will sound.

Singing bowls each have their own beautiful tone, it is important that you find the right bowl for you when you are looking to buy one. As with purchasing a bell the same principles apply to singing bowls—look for a bowl that is the right size for your hand and has the right sound for you. Make sure you get a chance to try the singing bowl before you buy it. Each bowl needs to be sold with its own pillow to rest on and a wooden mallet.

How to use your Singing Bowl

Take a deep breath in and breathe out, relax and focus on your intention. Think about what you would like to happen when you use your singing bowl, for example you would like to uplift your home and clear out any stale energy.

It is important that you wake your singing bowl up by striking it four times with the mallet once in the north, once in the south, once in the east and once in the west. When you are on the last strike you will need to carefully move the mallet around the bowl to create the humming sound. This can take practice so keep trying if it doesn't work the first time. Try to balance the singing bowl on top of your thumb and fingers.

Once you have woken the singing bowl up, carry the bowl around in your non-dominant hand, on its cushion if you want to, or just resting on your fingertips, while you strike the bowl with the mallet and move it around the outside of the singing bowl to create the beautiful sound. Remember to focus on your intention and start walking from your front door clockwise around each room in your home striking the singing bowl with the mallet and moving the mallet around until the sound finishes. Open the windows up in your home to let any stagnant energy out.

When you have finished walking around your home,

stand still and clear your own energy by striking the mallet against your singing bowl, feel the sound vibrate up and down your body.

Drums

The drum is a very powerful space clearing tool, just like bells and singing bowls can uplift and clear energy, drums can very quickly clear the energy and heal people in a room or space. The drum will bring balance to a home, it balances out the feminine and masculine energies.

Each drum has its own unique sound which can change depending on the weather and time of day, this is because drums are made out of animal skin which tightens or loosens according to the moisture in the air.

It is up to you what type of drum you would like to use to space clear, however I find that it is best if you use a traditional Native American style hand held drum because they create a beautiful sound and have a lot of positive energy attached to them if they are made with love and dedicated correctly.

The drum is a sacred tool for Native American people so it is important that you treat your drum with respect, it is not a toy.

How to use a Drum to Space Clear

Take a deep breath in, breathe out, hold your drum close to you and focus your intention on space clearing your home. When you are ready and you have your intention clear in your mind, allow energy to build inside you. Hold your drum by the tying strings at the back in your non-dominant hand.

You can use your dominant hand or a drum stick to hit the drum. Start drumming with two beats, like the sound of your heart beat, make sure that your wrist is relaxed when you hit the drum. Relax and find the energy inside you, find the rhythm that you need. The drumming sound is so powerful it will clear your energy as well as your home's energy.

Drum in the corner of each room. Remember to focus on your intention and start walking from your front door clockwise around each room in your home, drumming with your hand or drum stick. Keep drumming until you feel that the energy is clear, when you are finished hold the drum to your heart and feel yourself relax and become uplifted. Open the windows up in your home to let any stagnant energy out.

DE-CLUTTERING/CLEANING YOUR HOME

You have just read about some of the different tools available to help you to space clear your home but there is also another easy space clearing technique that you can do it—is to de-clutter and clean your home. When you clean and clear the clutter from your home you are allowing the positive energy to flow through your home, you will feel the energy change instantly within your home.

If you have too much clutter or too many items or objects in your home there will be pockets of stagnant energy. Stagnant energy clings to items that you do not use very often so it is important that you take note of what you use regularly and what you can get rid of or pack away.

How to De-clutter Your Home

The first step to de-cluttering and cleaning your home is to go through your items in your home. If you have any old items that are broken, cracked or not working it may be time for you to get rid of or fix these items. Remember when you get rid of old broken items you are making room for positive new energy to enter your home.

The second step is to sort through items in your home room by room when you can. This can be a big job so try to set aside time when you can do it, you do not have to de-clutter the whole house in one day. Focus on one room at a time so that you don't get overwhelmed. Have a pile of things that you definitely want to keep, a pile that you want to donate or give away to friends/family, a maybe pile and a throw out junk pile.

After you have put all of your items into piles it is important that you throw your junk items immediately, take your donation items and put them in your car if you have one or near the front door so that you remember to give them away. It is also important that you go through the maybe pile and be very clear about whether you need to or want to keep the item, if you don't need it or really want it throw it out or donate it to someone else. When you are ready put all of the things that you want to keep away in their own special places so that you can have your home clutter free and the positive energy can flow freely.

It is also important that you regularly clean your home to get rid of any dust, dirt or energy that has built up. By cleaning the floors, benches, windows and any other surfaces around your home you are actively space clearing your environment. This sounds like a normal thing for people to do but some people have become so busy in their everyday lives that they have forgotten the importance of doing simple things like cleaning and de-cluttering.

When you have finished cleaning your home you may like to use one of the space clearing methods in this book to finish clearing the energy around your home.

MUSIC

Music is great for the soul and a way to lift up energy in your home. When you play high vibrational music or music that makes you feel good it really can make a huge difference to how you feel and how your home feels as well. Nature based sounds such as birds singing, running water, the ocean and the sound of rain; or relaxation music such as Native American flute and drums, instrumental music or Tibetan monks chanting are all very popular types of music that can be played to uplift and clear the energy in your home.

Some people choose to play very loud powerful music such as opera or rock to blast out the negative energy from the home. You may choose to play your favourite music from a CD or on your mobile device. You could also play your own instruments at home or sing to lift up the energy and space clear your home. You may even like to hum, sing, chant 'Om' or sing 'Amen' when you are trying to clear the energy in your home.

It doesn't really matter which type of music or what sound you use, the most important thing is that you feel positive, empowered and can clearly state your intention of clearing your home while you have the music playing.

CLEARING THE ENERGY WITH POSITIVE THOUGHTS AND INTENTIONS

To space clear your home you can use some of the tools and techniques that I have written about in the previous pages such as using incense or sage to smudge your house, but if any of these tools or techniques do not suit you there is another way to space clear without using anything other than your own mind and positive intentions.

Some people who may be living away from home or who are not able to physically get home to space clear their home can do so from a distance by using their own mind to clear the energy in their home.

It is very easy to clear the energy in your home from a distance, all you need to do is focus on and see each room in your home. Imagine yourself walking through your home, go into each room and see yourself standing in the middle of the room.

When you can see yourself in each room imagine white light circling around the room and going into all of the corners of the room. As you imagine white light circling and clearing the energy in each room, ask in your mind for all negativity to be removed from that room. Visualize all of the white light moving out of the room through the doorways and out through the windows. You should then imagine that your whole home is now shining brightly with clean and clear bright white energy.

The Mountain Resort And The Spirit

I have had many experiences with space clearing homes, offices and even pieces of land but one of the most unexpected space clearing experiences occurred when I was running one of my spiritual retreats in a mountain resort. I used this resort a couple of times a year to run my weekend retreats, and on this one occasion I showed up to set up the normal smaller function room that I used to teach in. When I checked in to the resort I was told by the staff member that the function room had been converted into a restaurant, so I was shown to a bigger brighter room further away from reception.

On the first day of the retreat I spoke to a staff member from the resort, he asked me what kind of function I was running and I explained to him that it was a spiritual retreat about psychic development. When he found out what I was teaching he asked if he could speak to me away from my group. I was unsure what he would say but I agreed to talk to him away from the group.

When we went away from the group the staff member told me that he and some of the other staff members thought that there was a ghost in the resort, specifically in the old function room that is now the restaurant, they all felt scared in this room and this was the room where I was supposed to be teaching my retreat for the weekend.

This is was a great experience to be able to teach my students so I went to investigate with the staff member. As I walked into the dark room I could feel a strong male presence there, this was not a friendly energy he felt very angry and he had an old feeling about him. He was not happy about being disturbed and was not happy about all of these people changing the room around.

I left the room with the staff member and asked him what he and the other staff had experienced or felt in the room, I did not tell him what I initially felt or saw. He said that many of the staff were scared in that room because they felt like someone was watching them particularly when they were in the room by themselves.

A female staff member had set the function room up with tea light candles on each table, after the function was over she went into the room to tidy up, she blew out all of the candles and went into the kitchen. When she returned a minute later the room was lit up again with every candle buring on the tables, no one else was working in that area or would have had time to light all of the candles in such a short amount of time. The male staff member said this female was so freaked out she didn't want to work in that room anymore. He also said other staff members had experienced many different things including books jumping off the bookshelf at them in that room near the old stone fire place.

I asked the staff member if he wanted me to try and help clear this space. I said to him that I would need to have permission from the owner of the resort to do this. He checked with the owner and they were very open to me trying to help space clear the room as long as it was kept quiet and did not interfere with any of the staff or guests.

The retreat went on as usual and I taught the students about psychic protection and space clearing as well as many other things, but on the last day I asked the students if they would like to go into a room to feel its energy. They all agreed. I didn't tell them anything about the room or what had happened there, I wanted to see if they would be able to pick up on the old man's energy.

As soon as we entered the room a few of the students could feel a presence and some said they felt it was angry. A couple of them even pointed to the fireplace. After they revealed what they felt in the room I let them know what I had felt and what had been going on in the room. I told them that I would be space clearing this room and if they wanted to stay they could stay and help or if they wanted to leave that was OK as well. They all wanted to stay and help.

This was not something I had planned prior to arriving at the resort but it ended up being an great experience for the students to feel spirits and learn how to move negative spirits or energy on.

To clear the old man's spirit out of the room I began by spraying my protection spray which is a spritzer of essential oils, into each corner of the room. As I sprayed I asked for all negativity to be removed and I asked for protection for myself and everyone in the room.

After clearing the room with spray, I then asked for all of the students to hold hands, with me included, in a circle. I lit three candles and put them in the center of the circle and I asked all of the students to hold hands, to focus on the candles and ask for the spirit to be sent to the light. I called upon Archangel Michael and asked him to come and take this lost spirit to the light. I felt the old man resisting but I continued to ask three times, on the third time I felt a heat come over me and I felt that the male spirit had left.

As soon as the spirit left the room the energy was a lot

calmer and cooler. The students felt the change immediately. I explained to them that it was important that we snuff the three candles out, we were not to blow the candles out to make sure that the energy was not released.

Please note that sending this spirit to the light did not harm it, it actually helped him to grow spiritually and not be stuck in that room. The male spirit was getting frustrated being there because he didn't understand why so many strangers were in his room and moving things around.

This resort that I was teaching in was built on a massive piece of traditional farming land on top of a mountain. The resort's main office and function room were in the original cottage that had been renovated and converted. This male spirit may have been an original owner of the land or a drover or cattleman that had once lived there.

The owner of the resort and staff members are now much happier working in the converted function room which is now a busy restaurant, and I feel that the old male spirit is much happier as well having being reconnected with his family in spirit.

CHAPTER 4

HOW TO KEEP THE ENERGY POSITIVE IN A HOME

It is not only important to space clear your home it is also important that once you have lifted the energy in your home you maintain it and keep your home and everyone in it feeling positive. You can do this in a variety of ways such as fresh air, sunlight, green plants or by using the principles of Feng Shui, crystals, aromatherapy and much more. I have discussed a few of these topics earlier in the book and explained how to use them to space clear your home, I will now explain to you how to use some of these tools and techniques to keep the energy in your home free flowing, positive and uplifting.

FENG SHUI

What is Feng Shui?
Feng Shui is an ancient Chinese art form which was developed over 3,000 years ago to create harmony between

people and their environment and to enhance people's health and wellbeing. This is achieved by arranging the energy in and around the environment.

Feng Shui is used to create positive energy in all areas of the home, it involves gathering the good energy or 'chi' so that you can reduce the negative energy. Feng Shui shows that every living and non-living thing has its own energy. We are constantly coming into contact with all of these different energies everywhere we go, so it is important that we create a safe, positive space for ourselves in our home.

If you follow the principles of Feng Shui you will be able to balance the energy in each room of your home which will then help to promote good health and abundance for everyone who lives in your home. When you change the furniture placement and the surroundings in your home you lift the energy up which allows you to change your life for the better. In Feng Shui you need to look at your home as a whole system because each room and each part of the home is connected energetically to the other.

You do not need to be a Feng Shui expert to start applying the principles to your home. There are a lot of easy Feng Shui hints and tips that you can easily apply to your home straight away.

When you start to think about how to use Feng Shui to create positive energy in your home it can be helpful to identify which part of your home you think may need the most help or needs more positive energy. For example, you may already feel great about your lounge room and bedroom, but your spare room or home office may be in need of some extra positive energy or decluttering.

Look at how the Feng Shui energy, runs throughout your whole house. Do all of the rooms in your home have positive energy or the ability to maintain positive energy? Does the energy flow freely or does it get stuck before it reaches certain areas or rooms in your home? Make sure that you check even small spaces such as cupboards, sheds, attics and the laundry to see how the energy feels in there. If a house has positive energy flowing through and around it, anyone that lives or visits the house will feel uplifted and have a greater sense of well-being.

Once you have identified the rooms or areas that you would like to add positive energy to, you can start to make a list of where you would like to start implementing the Feng Shui principles. Remember, as I said earlier in this book, space clearing it is all about the intent that you put out to the Universe, you need have an intent that you want your home to feel positive, uplifted and abundant for all who live and visit there.

Here is some essential Feng Shui information that relates to all of the different parts of your home. This information can help you to keep the energy positive in your home.

The Front Door

It is very important that you have a very strong, visually attractive front door so that you can welcome good energy into your home. Your house will gain energy and nourishment from your front door, this is why the front door is called the 'Mouth of Chi'.

Your front door needs to be able to attract and help the flow of good Feng Shui energy into your home instead of making the energy weak or negative or pushing it away.

The Lounge Room

It is very important that you have good Feng Shui in your lounge because this is where you and your family and visitors may spend a lot of time. Your lounge should have good lighting, clean and clear air, have everything organized in its own place and be uncluttered. It is your home, though so you need to feel good about what is in your home and in your lounge, follow what feels right for you and your family.

To check the flow of energy in your lounge stand at the entrance to the room and see how the energy feels. Can you imagine seeing where the energy flows to? If you can, see if you can see anything that blocks the good Feng Shui. Is an obstacle in the room that may slow the energy down or block the energy from flowing freely, for example if water was to flow through your lounge room where would the water flow to?

When you arrange the furniture in your lounge room try to create a room that feels right for you and your family. You may aim for a room that makes everyone have a feeling of being positively connected, social and comfortable.

The Kitchen

In addition to the lounge room your kitchen may be another part of your home where you spend a lot of time socializing with your family and friends, it is also a very important part of your home because this is where you store your food and gain your nourishment from. The kitchen has been considered to be the heart of the home since ancient times;

use Feng Shui to make it a happy and healthy.

To maintain positive energy it is essential that you have good nutrition because good nutrition produces good energy which then makes good Feng Shui for your home and the people in it.

It is not only nutrition that we should focus on when looking at the energy of your kitchen, it is also important to look at how your kitchen feels. Is the kitchen well balanced and clutter free? Does the energy feel happy and positive in your kitchen?

There are various things that you should pay attention to when you are looking at the Feng Shui energy in your kitchen, they are as follows:

Δ *Keep your kitchen clutter free*

Δ *Try not to have too many items on your bench tops—this includes kitchen utensils, bowls, pots and electrical items*

Δ *Have fresh air in your kitchen with windows open to let natural sunlight in*

Δ *Place a green plant, fresh green herbs, flowers and a bowl of fruit in your kitchen*

The Bathroom and Toilet

Some people may not realize the importance of the bathroom and toilet areas in relation to their design, Feng Shui energy and location. Bathrooms and toilets are just as important as the kitchen, lounge and bedrooms. In fact it is especially important that you pay attention to these areas because they are associated with the water element and they do tend to leak energy. If you have a bathroom or toilet that is well maintained and has good Feng Shui energy you are creating a positive, calm and healing energy for your home.

One of the most important things for you to check for both the bathroom and the toilet is to make sure that there are no dripping taps and that all of the plumbing fixtures are clean and working well. If you have a dripping tap in Feng Shui it is believed to encourage you to waste money—the money is flushed down the drain.

There are various things that you should pay attention to when you are looking at the Feng Shui energy in your bathroom and toilet, they are as follows:

△ *It is important to make sure that you can keep warm in the bathroom in winter months, add heat lamps or try to make the space warm for the cooler months.*

△ *Try to have things that are visually pleasing to you, such as pictures or designs that you like.*

△ *The lighting is important in the bathroom particularly for women who need to do their makeup, so make sure you have adequate lighting. You may choose to have different lights for dimming or even candles to set a romantic mood in the bathroom.*

△ *Mirrors are important in the bathroom not only so you can see yourself but also to bring in good Feng Shui energy through the water element.*

The Bedroom

The bedroom is an extremely important room in the house, it is the room that you go to privately for rest, sleep, fun, passion and sensual energy. The bedroom is often hidden away from visitors so many people don't think it is important to look at this room, but it is essential for your own wellbeing and for your relationship area as well.

Everyone has their own taste in decoration and their own idea of what the perfect bedroom would be for them. In a bedroom that has good Feng Shui energy each item will reflect the clear positive intent for happiness, health, love and relaxation.

There are various things that you should pay attention to when you are looking at the Feng Shui energy in your bedroom from the lighting to the color scheme and also by looking at the bed that you sleep on and what items you have in your bedroom. The main things that you should pay attention to are as follows:

Fresh Air, Essential Oils, Scented Candles

It is sometimes easy to overlook the need for fresh air in a room, this is especially important for your bedroom. You will be spending many hours each night in your bedroom therefore it is very important that you have good clean air circulating in your bedroom. Try to let natural fresh air in if you can by opening up your windows. If your windows are always closed you can be breathing in air that is stale and the energy can become stagnant.

If you can't open the windows in your bedroom you may like to burn essential oils or scented candles to clear the air. Scented candles not only smell fantastic but they are also great energy for lighting the bedroom instead of using a normal bright electric light.

If you take time to use essential oils or to light a candle you can lift the energy in your bedroom and this will help you feel more positive and relaxed which will then help you to sleep better.

The Bed

When you are looking at the Feng Shui energy in your bedroom your bed is one of the most important pieces of furniture in your whole house, not just in your bedroom. Your personal energy is connected to your bed and the energy of your bed is directly related to your relationship area and your health and well-being.

Your bed should look good and feel good to you, it should be well-balanced, have a solid headboard, a good comfortable mattress and sheets, with pillows and blankets that you like and that are comfortable.

The placement of your bed in your bedroom is extremely important, if possible you should place your bed where you can easily access the bed from both sides. Try not to have the foot of your bed directly facing the door in the coffin position because this will not allow for a good night's rest.

Also try to have a solid wall behind your bed if you can, not under a window. If possible try not to place your bed in front of a big mirror or built in wardrobe with mirror doors because this can go against you and your partner's harmony and sexual energy. For balance it can be a good idea to have matching side tables, one on each side of the bed.

Bedroom Objects and Art

The objects and art that you have in your bedroom are very important because they affect the Feng Shui energy of your bedroom. It is important that you avoid any photos, paintings or images of people that are by themselves, lonely, sad, aggressive or violent because your bedroom is the place that you need to create positive relationship energy in.

Try to choose pictures and paintings of positive things for your bedroom, also have happy photographs of you and your partner it you have one, if not choose pictures of what you do want to manifest in your life, particularly in your relationship area.

Electronic and Exercise Equipment

Your bedroom should be a place of rest, relaxation and passion so it is important that you do not have too many pieces of electrical equipment in the bedroom such as a television, laptop, computer, tablet. The same thing applies to any exercise or work out equipment because all of these pieces of equipment do not have good Feng Shui energy when they are placed in a room that is meant to be used for rest, they do not allow for a good energy in your bedroom.

Lighting and Colors in the Bedroom

It is very important to have the right lighting in your bedroom. If possible you can use lamps, a light with a dimmer switch or have candles ready for use. It is good to have a choice of different kinds of light to create different moods and energy in the bedroom.

Just as the lighting is important in the bedroom so is the choice of your color scheme for the bedroom. It is important to have warm, soothing colors in your bedroom such as earth or skin color tones. Try not to have too many blues or water element colors in your room because you want to keep the colors warm and include some red colors in your room to promote passion and fulfilment in your relationship area. Try to choose colors that suit you and your family and that will work in well with your bedroom furniture and décor.

CRYSTALS

At the beginning of chapter three I covered the healing power of crystals and how to use crystal gridding to space clear and protect your home. There are many different types of crystals in the world and each has their own special healing powers. I will now cover some additional crystals that you can use to enhance the energy in your home to keep everyone feeling healthy and positive.

It is important that you learn what each crystal does so that you can use the right crystal to achieve the intention that you have, for example you should use rose quartz for love and relationships. You may like to wear the crystals in a pendant, as a bracelet, on a ring or have them in and around your home on display in bowls, in a crystal grid pattern, on a table or hang them as a sun catcher near your window.

Here is a list of some of the more common crystals that you can use in and around your home. I have focused on categorizing the crystals into groups. Each group relates to an emotional feeling or energy that you may want to achieve.

Balance

Life is very hectic, for most people it can be extremely hard to find balance between your work, family, friendships and relationship. Do you feel like you need to have better balance in your life? Or do you feel that your work and family life is balanced but you just need to find more time to balance your own mind, body and spirit?

It is hard to find balance in our lives when we are busy racing around during the day, which is why it is so important to create a positive environment at home, so you can recharge and rebalance yourself.

The following crystals can help you to uplift your energy and find balance in your life again:

Chrysocolla
Chrysocolla enhances positive energy and gets rid of any negative energy in and around a person. Chrysocolla helps to balance out a person's mind, body and spiritual energy.

To find your own sense of balance and to enhance your inner confidence and personal power wear Chrysocolla or place it in and around your home.

Turquoise
Turquoise is a wonderful balancer and healer, it helps people to balance out their energy and gives them a strong sense of peace and serenity. If you wear or hold a piece of turquoise you can uplift your energy, relieve your stress and bring positive energy into your life. You can also place turquoise in and around your home wherever you feel you would most benefit from it.

Watermelon Tourmaline
Watermelon tourmaline is a very powerful healing crystal which helps to balance out the male and female energies

within a person. It can also remove any stagnant, confused or angry energy to create a positive harmonious energy in an environment.

Watermelon tourmaline encourages people to have a calm, balanced energy and state of mind. You may like to wear a watermelon tourmaline piece of jewelry, pendant or necklace or place it in and around your home.

Change

Changes in your life are unavoidable; you may be on the verge of some big changes such a new job, having a baby, children leaving home, beginning to study, changing your relationship or moving home. Whatever the change is that is happening around you it is very important not to fear change, try to have a positive mindset and welcome in the new energy that comes with the changes in your life.

The following crystals can be very helpful in times of change:

Blue Aventurine

Blue aventurine is great for times of change because it is a powerful crystal that helps to increase your energy and give you a positive outlook on life. Blue Aventurine also has a calming effect on people's emotions, which is helpful for anyone who going through a process of change in their lives.

Fuchsite

Fuchsite is a wonderful crystal which helps people solve their problems, it also helps relieve emotional shock and enables people to feel positive and inspired. This is a very good crystal to have with you during times of change.

Communication

Communication is the key to any successful relationship, which is why it is so important to communicate correctly with our loved ones, friends, work colleagues and any other people that we come in contact with.

We communicate in various different ways including verbally, non-verbally, with sign language and by writing. It doesn't matter which form of communication you use, it is important that you communicate in a clear, concise and positive way so that other people can understand what it is that you want to convey to them.

If everyone in your home is communicating effectively with each other it will help to keep the energy positive in your home because there will be less conflicts or misunderstandings and more peace and happiness.

You can improve your communication and the communication of everyone else in your home by using some of the following crystals:

Blue Lace Agate

Blue lace agate is a calming, uplifting crystal, it encourages peaceful communication. Blue lace agate also helps to reduce family disagreements by helping people to communicate with each other and by calming the energy around the home.

Larimar

Larimar is a very soothing crystal which is great for helping people to express their emotions. Larimar releases any emotional blocks or attachments and allows people to open up to love and nurturing. This crystal is very good for helping people to communicate openly in a loving way that benefits everyone.

Energy

Many of us need more energy to do the things that we want to do during our busy days. There are some crystals which can help you feel reenergised and that can also help lift the energy in and around your home. These crystals can help you to feel more energetic, passionate, active and motivated.

The following crystals can help to bring you positive energy, passion and motivation:

Yellow Apatite

Yellow apatite is a great crystal that can get rid of many toxins in your body and also help get rid of any stagnant energy in and around your home. Yellow apatite also helps people to feel reenergized, passionate and motivated.

Tangerine Quartz

Tangerine quartz helps to energize you, it gives you motivation to move forward and an extra energy lift. Tangerine quartz can help with building and maintaining a sense of confidence that can then help to keep your energy high and keep you motivated. When your energy is positive and you feel motivated this energy then radiates out of you to everyone else in your home.

Happiness

Happiness is essential to a healthy life, if you can lead a happy and balanced life you and your loved ones will benefit from it. Everyone is individual, each person has their own likes and dislikes and things that make them happy. What makes one person happy may not make another person happy, we are all different.

It is really important that you find out what makes you happy so that you can continue to have positive energy around you. There are many different crystals that can help enhance the happiness in your life, they are as follows:

Citrine

Citrine brings positive energy, happiness and enthusiasm to anyone that is wearing it or to the space that it is placed in. It is also an abundance crystal so it brings in new finances, happiness and love and abundance in all good things in your life.

Citrine also helps to motivate by opening up people's creativity and by helping them to express themselves so that they can feel happy and at peace with their lives.

Peridot

Peridot is a very powerful crystal that cleanses your energy, reduces stress and opens your heart to happiness and new beginnings. Peridot also enhances your self-confidence and helps you to move forward and take responsibility for your life in a positive way.

Remember that crystals can help to heal you but it is still important that you stick to your regular medications and natural therapies which are recommended to you by qualified medical practitioners.

MALA BEADS

What are Mala Beads?

A mala is a strand of beads, traditionally used in Buddhist religious practices such as during meditation. A mala is usually made up of 108 beads that are strung together by strong string or elastic to create a necklace or bracelet. The mala beads are used in a similar way to the Roman Catholic rosary beads as they are used as focus point during prayers and meditation and they are also used for counting during mantra meditations.

Malas are always made with round, small beads that are usually 7–10mm in size. The mala beads are traditionally made from many different things such as bodhi seeds, wood, crystal gemstones, yak bones and lotus seeds. Each bead is shaped and made smooth to allow the user to easily move their fingers over the bead.

Many people who practice yoga and meditation use mala beads. Even if you don't practice these things mala beads can still be a very powerful focus point for you to put your positive intentions to. You may like to wear a mala necklace or bracelet or have it in your bedroom at home, this can help you to maintain the positive energy in your home.

How to use Mala Beads

If you are interested in learning how to use mala beads it is quite simple. The first thing that you need to do after getting your own set of mala beads is to focus upon finding the largest mala bead on your bracelet or necklace, this large bead is called the 'guru of the mala' and it is usually found in the middle of the bottom string of mala beads where the string is knotted or tied together.

Once you have found the guru mala bead, put the bead that is on the right of your guru mala bead between your middle finger and thumb. Take time on this first mala bead to focus on your breathing—breathe in and breathe out. The next thing to focus on is what you are trying to achieve, what is your intent. For example you may like to focus on having a positive and abundant energy in your home.

When you are ready, pass your fingers over each mala bead and focus your intention with each bead as it passes through your fingers. Remember that there are usually 108 mala beads on a string so you would be putting your intention into 108 beads and thinking positive thoughts each time (there are also mala beads that come in smaller numbers but the main one I am focusing on is the 108 mala). If you can do this on a regular basis think how positive the energy will be around you and your home.

If you wish to keep the positive energy and intentions with you throughout the day you may choose to wear your mala beads as a necklace, bracelet or put them in a special pouch that keeps them protected in your wallet or bag.

If you choose not to wear your mala beads when you are not using them that is OK, you may like to put the mala beads in a special place that is safe, or you can put them on display on a special sideboard or altar which may have many other positive objects of yours on it.

The most important thing to do with your mala beads is to treat them with respect and keep your positive intentions going when you are holding them.

MEDITATION

Meditation is a great stress reducer and a great way to relax and quiet your mind, it not only helps you feel more positive about life it can even help you psychologically and physically. There are many other benefits that meditation can bring, it can help you to remain calm and positive, it can help you to focus better on your work or studies and it can even help you to relax your mind for a better sleep.

To some people who have never had a chance to meditate before it can seem a bit daunting, but I can assure you that there are many different forms of mediation and it is actually quite simple. You do not need to be a Buddhist monk or a yoga master to be able to meditate, all you need is approximately ten minutes in a quiet space by yourself to start off with.

There is no set time that you must stick to if you want to meditate, you can meditate at any time of the day that suits you. You may like to meditate as soon as you wake up in the morning to start your day, or at lunch time to give you positive energy to continue your day, or even at the end of the day to help you relax before you go to sleep.

There are many different meditation techniques but I will just give you a few examples here, it is up to you what type of meditation technique you would like to use. You may like to try a few different techniques to see what suits you best. Remember that it is not hard, the whole purpose of meditation is to calm your thoughts so that you can have positive energy and inner balance.

How to Meditate Quickly and Easily

There are a few easy steps that you can take to start meditating, they are as follows:

1. *Take some time out of your day, try to set aside approximately ten minutes when you won't be disturbed by anyone.*
2. *Go to a quiet place where you know that you won't be disturbed while you meditate, it may be an office room, your bedroom or even outside in a park or garden.*
3. *Sit or lie comfortably.*
4. *Focus on your breathing, breathe in and out in long deep breaths. Focus on relaxing all the muscles in your body.*
5. *Calm your mind and let go of anything that is stressing you or making you upset. Be present only in the moment, try not to think about all of the chores or work that you*

need to do that day.

6. *See yourself shining brightly, full of white light from the tips of your toes all the way to the top of your head. Imagine that you are a clear vessel with white light pouring out of every part of your body. After you see yourself shining brightly, imagine that you are surrounded by a big bubble of gold light. This gold light will protect your energy and allow you to remain positive.*

7. *After you have surrounded yourself in gold light, focus on your breathing again, think about all of the things that you are thankful for in your life. Smile and bring your awareness back to your physical body and the area that you are meditating in.*

8. *When you are feeling happy and relaxed, stretch your arms up above your head, shake your hands and feet to get the energy flowing and enjoy the positive relaxed energy that is flowing throughout your body.*

If you can try to practice meditating on a regular basis you will notice how much it will improve your life.

GRATITUDE AND POSITIVE ATTITUDE

You may be wondering why I am writing about gratitude in a book about clearing the energy in your home. The answer is simple, your own personal energy affects everyone and everything in your home. If you are upbeat, positive and grateful everybody in the home benefits from it.

It is important that you try and practice gratitude every day. It doesn't matter what religion or belief system you have, if you don't take time to be grateful you will never have more happiness in your life. If you are grateful you will be given more happiness and you will have more abundance in your life.

Gratitude and a positive attitude to life can change all the areas in your life from your financial situation to your health, your career and your relationship area.

Are You Grateful?

How do you feel about the following areas: your family, career, relationships, health and finances?

Is there an area where you feel you could add more positive energy?

Is there an area where you feel it is already going really well and you feel that it is a positive area that you are grateful for? Have you considered that maybe this area is going so well for you because you are already grateful for it? An example of this may be your relationship area—you may be thankful and grateful for your partner every day and as a result of this positive energy and gratitude you will receive even more positive energy in your relationship.

When you are feeling grateful and have a positive attitude for the people and things in your life, you will attract more of these people and things to be grateful for. It is important that you try not to focus in on the negative things that are occurring in your life, because energy flows where your attention goes. If you are thinking of negative things you may manifest and make negative things happen.

There are so many little things and big things to be grateful for every day. I am always grateful for the roof over my head for myself and my family and for the food that we have to eat that sustains and nourishes us.

What are you grateful for? It can be an uplifting and positive experience to write down a list of thing that you are grateful for. Here are some examples of things that you may like to write down:

Δ *I am grateful for my job because it gives me the finances to provide for myself and my family.*

Δ *I love my friends and family and I am grateful for having them in my life.*

Δ *I have so much energy and I am grateful that I can enjoy running, walking and exercising to keep my body fit and healthy.*

Δ *Today is a great day and I am grateful because we are all happy and healthy.*

Gratitude and Your Relationships

Gratitude and a positive attitude make relationships flourish. If your relationship area is shining brightly you will be full of positive energy and this energy will radiate out of you to every person that you come into contact with. It will also help your home have a positive feel about it.

Gratitude and Your Health

Your relationship area is not the only area that you should focus your gratitude and positive attitude on. Your health and your family's health is the other area that is extremely important.

Try to be thankful and grateful for every part of your body and your health. When you are grateful for your body you will notice a change in your energy and the way that you see yourself, you may not be so quick to judge what you look like or be so hard on yourself about your physical appearance.

When you feel grateful you will begin to feel more positive about your life, this in turn will influence how other people relate to you and how you relate to them.

Gratitude for Your Finances and Work

Another area that would benefit from you having a positive attitude and gratitude is your financial and work area. This can be a difficult thing to do if you don't currently have a job, are in financial difficulty or you are currently in a job that you are unhappy in.

In these cases the most important thing to do is to start thinking about something positive that you can be grateful for. For example you may be grateful that you have enough money today to pay your rent or your mortgage and to have enough food in your home to eat.

Remember you want to focus on the positive things in your life that you can be grateful for, not the negative things or things that you don't yet have.

If you can have a positive attitude and be grateful in some or all of these areas in your life you will be well on your way to creating a much more positive energy for yourself, everyone in your home and your life.

SUNLIGHT/NATURAL LIGHTING

Have you ever noticed that you feel drained after being at work or other places where you are constantly stuck under fluorescent lighting? Do you sometimes go hours without being able to see the sky or feel the sun on your face? If you have answered yes to one or both of these questions you are not alone, this is becoming a common thing for people who are leading very busy lives.

Some people are becoming so disconnected from the natural world, including the sun and sky, they are forgetting the importance of natural sunlight. The sun reenergizes us, warms us and brightens up our energy, it also provides us with natural lighting and vitamin D. Vitamin D is essential for our bodies because it helps the body absorb calcium and phosphorus which are two very important minerals for bone and tooth growth.

There are many people who are deficient in vitamin D because they do not have access to natural sunlight, this can sometimes be due to where they live, such as people who live in very cold climates in the Northern Hemisphere. Other people who may be deficient in vitamin D are the elderly, sick, people who wear full head and body coverings and people who have very dark skin.

If someone is deficient in vitamin D this can lead to S.A.D, seasonal affective disorder, this is quite common in people who don't get enough sunlight in the winter months and it can lead to depression.

If you live in an area where you do get enough sunlight make the most of it. Too much sun is not a good idea, though, because of skin cancer and sunburn, but a bit of sunlight is required each day for us to remain healthy.

Try to open your blinds, curtains and windows to let the sunshine come into your home. By letting the sunshine in you are recharging the energy in your home and you are adding positive energy as well. If you can't access windows easily, try to get outside and put your face up to the sun for a few minutes each day, you will instantly feel your energy lift.

HIMALAYAN ROCK SALT LAMPS

Himalayan rock salt lamps not only look beautiful they are wonderful for helping attract and keeping positive energy in the home. Himalayan rock salt lamps also have amazing healing properties. The healing energy from these lamps is claimed to help with mental health disorders, colds, headaches and respiratory problems. These lamps are natural, they are made up from salt that came from oceans which are millions of years old. The Himalayan salt is pure and it is found in salt beds that are deep inside the Himalayan Mountains.

Himalayan rock salt lamps are nature's best ioniser, this is because the way that the lamp works is similar to a man-made ioniser. The salt lamp needs to be heated for its healing properties to work. When the lamp is turned on and heats up it attracts water molecules from the air which then bind the negative ions with the excess positive ions. Some examples of positive ions are electrical smog, cigarette smoke, pollution, bacteria and dust. Negative ions are purely natural ions that can be found in nature. You can find pure negative ions in the air after storms, if you are near the ocean, near waterfalls and various other natural places.

When the negative ion connects with the positive ion it gets rid of the positive ion therefore cleaning and clearing the air. Himalayan salt lamps can also help to reduce radiation so it is a good idea to put a salt lamp near your electrical devices. Electrical devices are all around us at work and at home. Most people have televisions, computers, laptops, air conditioners or heaters, telephones or mobile phones and digital music players. Each of these items create positive ions which is known as 'electric smog'.

Electric smog is when the energy in the air deteriorates, and this can lead to many health problems. Many people may not even be aware of how much electrical smog is around them and their home. Think about your home, do you have a television set, laptop, digital music player, air conditioner and mobile phone running in your bedroom while you are in there? Is all of this electrical equipment running when you are trying to sleep? Electric smog can definitely affect you in a negative way both mentally and physically.

The Himalayan salt lamp can help to clear the electric smog by increasing the number of negative ions in a particular area in your home. You can also open the windows regularly in your home to let the fresh air and sunlight in.

You can put a Himalayan salt lamp anywhere in your home that suits you, but here are some of the best locations to lift the energy up and to clear the air:

Δ *In the bedroom.*
Δ *In the lounge or living room near the television, it will add a soft beautiful light to the room as well as being functional.*
Δ *In the home office near any electrical devices such as*

*computers, laptops and air conditioners. Be aware though
that the salt lamp attracts moisture so it does leak a bit of
water when not turned on, so please do not put it on top of
any electrical appliance or surface that is not waterproof.*

FRESH AIR

You have just read about electric smog and positive ions in the
air, and as simple as it sounds many people underestimate
the importance of fresh air in and around the home. It is
extremely important that you have good quality, clean air to
breathe. If there is dust or dirt lying in and around the home
this can not only cause health problems such as asthma it
can also create stagnant energy in the home.

Good ventilation in the home is just as important as having
a good source of natural sunlight. If possible, and if the air
quality outside is good and the weather is permitting, you
should try to open your windows regularly to let fresh air
into your home.

Many people use air conditioners and heaters which
recycle the old air in and around the home, this is not good
to do all the time. If you do use an air conditioner or heater
regularly remember to keep the filters clean and regularly
check that the devices are safe and providing clean air for
you and everyone in your home.

If you need to you can use air vents and fans to try and
move the stagnant air around in your home. Plants are also
good for cleaning the air in your home. Stagnant air is not
good for your health and it is not good for the energy in your
home. Flowing fresh air is the best air to have circulating

around your home, it helps to keep the energy positive in your home.

NATURE/INDOOR PLANTS

Plants are a wonderful addition to your home, you may like to focus on having indoor plants or have plants outside in your garden. As I have described earlier, the color green has a healing energy and indoor house plants are a great way to add color and positive energy to the home.

Plants not only add to a room they also clear the air and create a healthy environment. The ancient art of Feng Shui shows us that there are many plants that you can use inside your home to balance out and attract positive energy. There are specific plants that are recommended because of the shape and texture of their leaves. Plants which have round, soft leaves attract more positive energy into your home.

Try to avoid indoor plants that have spiky or pointy leaves because sharp points are not good for the energy flow around your home. Also try to avoid dried flowers or fake plastic flowers, if possible it is best use real flowers.

There are specific rooms in your home that will greatly benefit from having plants in them, they are: the entrance to your home—both inside and outside, the verandah/balcony, the lounge room, the kitchen and the dining room. You can even have indoor plants in your bathroom if that suits you. The best plants to have in your bathroom are plants that don't mind moisture or heat.

Some of the best indoor plants are:

Aglaonema

The aglaonema plant is a good looking plant that is slow growing and long lasting, they have large, narrow oval leaves on short stems. It's important to keep these plants warm and moist.

Bamboo

The bamboo plant is very good to have in your home, it brings in very good Feng Shui energy. Please see the separate section below on bamboo for more information.

Begonia

The begonia plants are some of the most popular indoor plants, there are many different types of begonia plants. Begonias cannot handle very cold temperatures, too much moisture or strong sunlight.

Croton

The croton plant is made up of a variety of beautiful bright colors such as bright reds, oranges, pinks, purples and yellows. The croton plant prefers warm, humid conditions with lots of water and dappled sunlight.

Ficus

The ficus tree is a very decorative plant that can be potted and kept indoors. The ficus tree needs warmth, humidity and lots of light. These plants do not like to be moved.

Orchids

Orchids are very popular and are beautiful plants which have a variety of different shaped and colored flowers. Orchids attract very good energy and fertility into your home.

Primrose

Potted indoor primrose plants are a wonderful way to attract positive energy into your home. The primrose plant comes in many different beautiful colors and is made up of many delicate flowers.

African Violets

African violets are very popular indoor plants, these plants come in many different colors and leaf forms. African violets love bright, warm and humid conditions.

Lucky Bamboo

Bamboo is a beautiful green plant that is very tough and hard wearing, it is great to have in a small pot indoors because it is very easy to look after and can live for a long time if cared for correctly. In Feng Shui a little bamboo plant is considered to bring good luck.

Bamboo Plants

When choosing your bamboo plant there are a few things that you may like to look at to increase the positive energy and good luck in your home. It is a good idea to try and have the five elements present in your bamboo and bamboo pot. The five elements are fire, water, wood, metal and earth.

You can easily apply all five elements by using the bamboo

and pot, for example the bamboo can be planted in a glass or metal pot. If you use a different kind of pot you can add the metal element by tying a coin to it. The earth element is the dirt or rocks which the bamboo is planted in and the water element is taken care of when you water the bamboo. The fire element can be linked in with the metal element, for example if you tie a metal coin to the pot you could use a red ribbon to secure the coin. The color red is associated with the fire element.

You don't need to go into so much detail and have all of the five elements for your bamboo plant it you don't want to. I have used a simple little piece of lucky bamboo plant in a clear glass jar with distilled water in it over the years and it has worked very well.

Scented Indoor Plants

There are some plants that have their own beautiful, unique fragrances which can help to clear the air in and around the home. Some fragrances and scents can create a balanced and harmonious energy. In Feng Shui certain scents can have a very positive and powerful effect on the energy in your home.

Here is a list of some of the best scented indoor plants and the energy that each of these plant's fragrances can bring to your home:

Miniature Roses—have the highest positive vibration of all plants
Rosemary—is for healing and protection
Lavender—is for relaxation, calming and inner peace

Basil—is for happiness, love and passion

Lemon—is for friendship and purification

Jasmine—is for love and money

Orchids—are for love and friendship

Juniper—is for cleansing

Sage—is for protection

Citrus—is cleansing

Eucalyptus—is for balance and cleansing

Fragrant Fresh Flowers

You may choose to have fresh flowers in your home to lift the energy up and to add color. Fresh flowers instantly add great energy to your home. It doesn't matter which flowers you choose it is a personal preference in regard to the color, shape, texture and scent of the flowers that you like.

When you do have fresh flowers make sure that you look after them by having them sit in clean water. Once the flowers are dying, limp or dried out it is important that you throw them out and clean out the old stale water so that you don't encourage any stagnant energy.

ESSENTIAL OILS

Essential oils are not only used to space clear a home as covered earlier, they are also used to lift the energy in a home and to help attract and maintain positive energy. Many essential oils can have a very positive affect on how we feel, by sensing and smelling the different oils you can uplift your own energy and the energy of everyone else in your home.

Each person has different likes and dislikes, what you may find pleasing to your senses may not appeal to someone else. It is important that you choose your essential oils wisely, ask the other people that live in your home if they like the smell of the oils that you have chosen before you burn them. If you burn oils that have a smell that the other people don't like it will cause negative energy not positive energy.

There are many different types of essential oil that you can buy, make sure that you buy a good quality pure oil. Here is a list of the more popular essential oils which you can use to help lift the energy up in your home:

△ *Apple*

△ *Bergamot*

△ *Cedarwood*

△ *Cyprus*

△ *Frankincense*

△ *Geranium*

△ *Jasmine*

△ *Lavendar*

△ *Lemon/Citrus*

△ *Neroli*

△ *Peppermint*

△ *Rose*

△ *Sage*

△ *Ylang Ylang*

Before you use any of these oils make sure that you learn or find out about the oils that you intend to use. Read any warnings or contraindications associated with that particular oil before you use it, particularly

if you or someone in your home is pregnant or has a specific allergy.

FOOD

Good food and water is essential not only to keep our body alive and strong it is also very important for us socially so we can bond with other people. Food has its own energy, what you eat can definitely affect the way you feel.

The quality of the food you eat is also important. When you are trying to keep yourself feeling happy and healthy take time to look at the food and drinks that you put into your body. Everybody has different likes and dislikes so what makes a great meal for one person may not suit another person. Also remember that each person has different dietary requirements, each body can tolerate different things.

It is important that you listen to what your body is trying to tell you, for example how does your body feel after you eat a hot curry dish? Does it feel good or do you feel like it doesn't agree with you?

Just as food is important for you physically it is also important to the energy in the home. If you have old, stale, expired food lying around on your bench tops, in your cupboards or in your fridge, this sends out negative energy.

Try to have fresh fruit and food that is still within its expiry date. Clear out any food that is off, old or out of date as soon as possible so that you can remove any old stagnant energy. When you remove this old food it makes way for you to add new food into your home, it also declutters your cupboards and fridge so you have more space.

It is not only important to pay attention to clearing any old food out of your home it is also important to have gratitude for your food. You can do this by being thankful for your food, by saying a prayer or blessing if that is your belief or just by savouring your food and not being wasteful.

Try to only cook the amount of food that you need, if you do have any extra left over food don't waste it—freeze it or eat it the next day. I know this may sound like a contradiction to what I previously said about throwing out old food but this food is fresh and still has good energy. This is a simple thing that many people do, but there are some people that are so busy that they forget to do these things. Some people have become accustomed to being in a throwaway society, they throw things out and waste good food without thinking about it.

Growing Your Own Food

Another great way to add positive food and energy to yourself, your family and your home is by growing your own foods. You may have space in your yard to have a vegetable, herb or fruit garden, or you may live in an apartment with space only for a small planter box of herbs.

It doesn't matter about the quantity of what you grow, it is the positive energy behind growing your own quality food that matters. It can be a great feeling to plant your own seedlings or seeds and watch them grow. After they grow you can enjoy the benefit of eating your own homegrown herbs, vegetables and fruit.

If you don't have the time or space to grown your own herbs, fruit or vegetables you may like to buy some fresh herbs from the grocery store and keep them in a jar with some water in it in your kitchen.

The smell of fresh herbs and the taste of them when you use them in your cooking is fantastic. This all brings a great energy into your kitchen and home and your body also benefits from it as well.

COLORS IN YOUR HOME

Many people may not be aware that the color scheme and different colored items in your home make a difference to how it feels. Have you ever walked into a home or place that has very dark purple, dark gray or black walls throughout it? If you have how did it make you feel?

Each person has their own taste when it comes to decorating, generally speaking if a room or the inside of a home is painted in really heavy dark colors it can make the room feel heavy, smaller and can hold onto negative or stagnant energy. It is OK to have a feature wall in dark colors, or to have darker furniture, just try to balance the darker color out with lighter walls around it.

To attract and keep the energy positive in your home, it is a good idea to use lighter colors or even a shade of white that you may like. However, as I have said with the dark colors it is just as important to make sure that you don't have too much white in your home. Too much white can make a home feel very clinical, like a hospital. It can also be hard to relax if there aren't any other colors around that your eye can focus on.

If you do have a lot of white in your home try to make

sure that you have different colored artwork, furniture or soft furnishings such as pillows, rugs, curtains or carpet. You don't need to just stick to having white colored walls, there are so many beautiful colors out there. Try to see what colors you are intuitively drawn to and see what suits your furniture, décor and your home.

Each color has its own unique energy that it brings into your home. When selecting the colors for your home it is a good idea to try and think about what energy you want in that room. Or you may want to focus on a particular part of your life that you want to enhance or attract new energy into. If you want to focus on a particular part of your life try to select colors that draw that energy to you, for example if you wanted to attract a relationship into your life you may choose to add some red features into your bedroom. I have written more about this in the Feng Shui section earlier in the book.

When you are looking at selecting the colors for a particular room remember that everything needs to be done in balance. If you overdo a color you can accidently end up with too much of that energy which then can be counterproductive to what you were originally trying to achieve.

Here is a list of some of the main colors that people have in their homes and the energy that they can bring:

Blues
The lighter shades of blue are usually are quite relaxing, peaceful and calming. Just remember though that you don't want to overdo it too much with one color. Too much blue, especially the darker shades, can have the reverse

affect energetically, it can make people feel depressed and lethargic.

As mentioned earlier in the Feng Shui section of the book, try not to have too much of the color blue in your bedroom because it can bring in too much of the water element. In the bedroom it is better to have the red fire passion element.

Reds

There are many different shades of red from maroon right up to tomato red or even some dark pinks and fuchsias. The color red is associated with passion, romance and action. This color is great in small amounts to attract positive energy.

Try not to overdo it with the red colorings because if you have too much red it equals too much passion which can then attract anger and or aggression. Red is fantastic to use in your bedroom as it is great for your intimate relationship area. Pinks can also be good in small amounts but it is obviously up to each person's personal taste.

Purples

Purple is a mixture of red and blue, it holds great energy for protection, spiritual connection and it is very luxurious. There are many different shades of purple from very light lilac right up to a very dark purple.

Balance is very important so if you are using a dark purple in your home try to stick to using it on a feature wall because too much purple, particularly if it is dark, can have a depressive or stagnant energy.

Greens

Green is such a beautiful healing color, it reminds us of nature and it attracts in healing and abundance energy. All shades of green are very positive, some people prefer a light mint green others may like dark emerald green.

If you don't want to paint your walls green you can add green plants or décor to your home to attract in positive energy. Be aware though, because too much green can attract in a lazy, sleepy energy. It is OK if you break the green up in different parts of your home. Try not to have plants in your bedroom if your room is small because it is not good Feng Shui, but if bedroom is a very large room then it is ok.

Oranges/Brown Earth Tones

Brown earth tones and shades of orange can bring in a very warm, positive grounded energy into your home. You do not have to have these colors painted on your walls, you may have polished wooden floors, wooden furniture or have artwork, furnishings or objects which have earthy brown and orange tones to them.

It is a good idea to have lighter colored walls with heavier earth toned wooden flooring or a lot of wooden furniture. If there is too much wooden furniture, brown earth tones or orange colorings it can make people feel heavy or restless.

Yellows

Yellow is such a bright, happy color it is a wonderful way to attract positive energy into your home. Yellow is also associated with creativity and inspiration.

Just as the sun brightens up dark spaces, the color yellow

can do the same thing. Try to use the yellow color in balance so that you don't cause the energy in the home to become restless.

Painting Your Home and Moving Items Around

It is amazing how different the energy in a home can become when you change the colors of the rooms or change the color of the furniture or soft furnishings. When you paint a room even if you repaint it the same color as it already is you are creating clean, new energy. The room will feel and look clean and the energy will be high and positive.

If you are renting you may not be able to change the color of the walls or paint them but you can add posters, paintings, curtains or change the furniture around. Sometimes even the smallest item or piece of color added to a room can lift the energy up enormously.

MANDALAS

What is a Mandala?

A mandala is a spiritual picture which is made up of sacred geometry and specific spiritual images and intentions which are put into it to attract positive energy. The picture is usually inside a circle, which is where the word mandala comes from—it is the Sanskrit word for circle. Some mandalas are created using geometric shapes, but all are formed around a center point.

A mandala is more than just a circular picture, it represents wholeness and the divine, our relationship to the infinity in our universe. Mandalas are found all around the world in many different spiritual traditions and belief systems. Some of examples of mandalas that are created with specific spiritual meaning are found in the zodiac wheel, the Native American medicine wheel, the Aztec calendar, the Tibetan Buddhist Mandalas and the Taoist yin and yang symbol.

It doesn't matter what the person's belief system or culture is, mandalas are a symbol of connection with intention, this connection is a visual connection between the person their intention and the mandala. The mandala helps the person to focus on a center point. Mandalas not only look beautiful and help with putting positive intention into your home they are also great to use as a meditation tool.

How to Create your own Personal Mandala

You can create your own mandala with images and colors that reflect what is important to you. You may like to use sacred geometry in your mandala or you may like to just use various patterns or colors that resonate with you. Try to gather together anything that you find inspiring, uplifting and positive—these may be your favorite photos, pictures or even your favorite patterns, shapes or colors.

Once you have found all of the different things that you want to add to your mandala it is time to combine all of these things together to make a picture or a pattern. Remember though that mandalas are always in the shape of a wheel or circle with a focus point in the middle so when you put your mandala together try to keep that structure in mind.

Each mandala is personal, it needs to resonate with you. If you don't feel like you are able to create your own mandala you may like to have someone else help you create one or you can buy one that resonates with you.

How to use a Mandala for Positive Intention

Once you have created your own mandala or have found one that suits your intention you can then begin to use it for meditation and for creating a positive intention in your home.

To use a mandala for positive intention or meditation try to find a time where you won't be disturbed, go to a quiet place where you can relax. When you are relaxed put your mandala on your lap in front of you, be clear about what your intention for this specific mandala is, what do you want to focus on. In this exercise we are focusing on bringing positivity into your home and into your life.

Breathe in through your nose, and out through your mouth, keep your eyes open and try to focus on your mandala, let your gaze be gentle and soft. Don't strain your eyes, just relax and allow yourself to blink normally. Use your mandala as a visual reference point, it will help you to meditate and it will give you positive energy.

Enjoy this moment, relax and focus on your positive intentions. Think of everything that is positive in your life, also try to focus on the positive things that you would like to welcome into your life. It can take time to learn how to meditate or use a mandala but the more you practice meditating with your mandala, the easier it will become. Try to meditate or use your mandala whenever you feel that you need some positive energy or if you want to have some time out to recharge and relax.

You may like to put your mandala on display in your bedroom or in your home, or you may like to have it put away in a special place that is just for you, it is up to you what works best.

PEOPLE AND PETS

People you have In and Around your Home

It may sound like common sense but the people that you have around you and your home does make a difference to the energy in your home. Obviously you can't change who your family members are, but you can change who you allow into your home and the energy that they bring with them. You can choose who you allow to affect your positive energy.

There will always be people who are quite negative or draining in your life. It is important that you pay attention to who these people are. If you know who the draining people are around you, you can make sure that you smudge your home or burn incense or essential oils after they have left so that you can clear their negative energy out of your home.

The reverse is true too, if you know that you have some friends or family members who are very positive, happy and fun people to be around, try to spend as much time with them as you can. Enjoy being around like-minded positive people because like attracts like and you will be attracting the positive energy to yourself as well as helping them to remain positive.

Try to be really conscious about who you are allowing to enter your private space, your home is your sanctuary. If people do not respect your wishes for privacy or respect what your belief systems are you do not have to allow these people into your home. It is important that you set clear boundaries for people, say no if you need to.

If you live with other people in a house or have flatmates it is very important that strict guidelines and rules are put down that all in the house know about and can follow. If there are no guidelines or rules it can make the house feel disjointed or housemates can accidently cause friction or angst without realizing it.

Each person needs to have their own say about what they will and won't put up with in the home and this is also in regard to who can visit; who can have visitors that stay overnight, who does what chores, what happens with bill paying, food and cooking. These things may seem like small issues to think about but they can become quite stressful and can feel bigger than they really are if they are not addressed properly, especially if housemates do not understand what is expected of them.

The most important thing to remember is that it is really important to have good, positive energy around you, your family and your home. Try to keep your energy positive and fill your life with as many positive people that you can.

Pets

People are not the only energies in a home, some families have pets as well. Usually when you have a pet in the home you are surrounded by unconditional love. Pets are also great to help you relax and to keep you company if you are lonely, they are great healers. Many animals are called upon to help people who have special needs such as the guide dogs dogs for the visually impaired or hearing dogs for people who are hearing impaired. Even if you don't have special needs it doesn't mean that you can't benefit from having a loving pet in your family and home.

Pets that are good natured and well trained are a great way to bring positive energy into your home, that is of course if you like pets and are not allergic to them. Pets can lift the energy of everyone who is in the home. You don't specifically need to have a dog or cat, you may like to have pet fish or even a pet bird or reptile, it just depends what suits you and your family and your home and lifestyle.

To maintain the positive energy in the home it is important that each member of the household is OK with having a pet, because if a pet is not wanted by a family member or is behaving aggressively or misbehaving a lot it can cause stress and negative energy in the home. If this is occurring in your home you may need to look at what your options are with the pet, can you get some advice from a vet or animal behavioral expert to help to train the pet or can you come to some solution or compromise with the person who doesn't like the pet.

To keep the energy in your home positive it is important that you keep the pet's bedding, toys, food and water bowls clean and clear. Also try to remove any pet hair or feathers that have been shed so that you keep your home clean and the air clean and clear as well.

Ochres, Oranges And New Paint Work

Color schemes in your home are key and it is very important to try and keep the paint fresh and clean in and around the space. I painted and changed the color scheme in my lounge, kitchen and entry area a few months ago and the difference it made to the energy in my home was incredible.

The areas of the home that my family and I use the most are the kitchen, lounge, bathroom and entry area to our home so I focused on painting these areas first. The colors in these areas were very outdated as I had painted it about seven years earlier when it was trendy to have bright feature walls. I had a burnt orange color in my kitchen and an ochre yellow color on the walls in the lounge room and entry space. These colors are nice but they were outdated, tired and stagnant. These rooms have seen a lot of changes over the past seven years and it was time to reinvigorate the space and breathe new life into the rooms.

After I changed the color scheme to a nice clean shade of white on the walls with a cream or off white color for the ceiling and window and door frames, I noticed that the house felt completely different. The energy was clean and clear and all the past stagnant energy had been removed.

To add color to my white walls I put up some hand painted artwork which come from my partner's family (his uncle painted one of the paintings). The colors that are in these paintings are the same orange, red, ochre and yellow colors that I had on my wall previously, but they stand out a lot more by having the white background of the walls.

Ever since I painted the walls in my home everyone who has visited has commented how the home feels different. Even my children and my partner have said that our home feels a lot lighter and the energy feels more positive. If you want to have a quick fix in your home, paint the walls and you will notice the new energy instantly.

CHAPTER 5

HOW TO SPACE CLEAR YOUR HOME TO SELL IT FAST

FENG SHUI

If you plan to or a trying to sell your house there are some important Feng Shui tips that you can use to help sell your home faster. When using the principles of Feng Shui you can easily analyze what does and doesn't make your home feel inviting, positive and appealing to people.

It is important to realize, though, that Feng Shui principles alone will not sell your home, there are other important things that you need to have. The first is a good real estate agent who knows the market well and can create a marketing plan that will draw potential buyers to you as well helping you find the right price to sell your home for.

There are many things that you can do to clear the energy in your home, as covered earlier in the book, but here are some additional hints to help you sell your home fast.

Take Note of what your Home Looks Like from the Outside

Imagine that you are a buyer or someone that has never met you or been to your house before, what do you think your home looks like from the outside? Remember first impressions last and it only takes a few seconds for a person to decide what they think about the appearance of your home.

Be honest with what you see, try to take the emotions out of it when you look at your home. You need to take into account the styles and current trends of the time, what may have been fashionable five to ten years ago may now be outdated and could possibly turn potential buyers off.

Go with the adage less is more, try to steer away from too many bright colors because potential buyers want to be able to see the home as a blank canvas to which they can then add their own sense of style to make it their own home.

Gardens and Landscaping

If you have a home that has a garden or lawn area it is very important that you pay attention to maintaining this area. Maintenance is the key! If you can afford to invest in some landscaping it can add some great energy and value to your home.

For the people who don't have a front yard or garden and who live in a townhouse, unit or villa, try to make the entry to your home appealing with potted plants or flowers. You could even purchase a new front door mat to add positive, welcoming energy when people arrive at your front door.

Another tip is to make sure that the number on your house or letter box is clearly visible so that people can find your home easily.

De-clutter Your Home

To keep the energy positive in your home try to create a place that feels spacious. You can do this by removing any excess clutter including extra pieces of furniture, knick knacks or photographs.

Potential buyers need to be able to connect with your home and visualize where they will put their own personal belongings. If a home is full of too many personal items or too many family photographs it can be hard for a buyer to connect and feel like they would belong there.

It is also important that the energy moves freely around the home and between the rooms in the home. If you have a spare bedroom or room that is full of junk, make sure that you store those items away neatly in boxes or you may even like to store them offsite at a storage facility just while you are in the process of selling your home.

It's also a good idea to limit how many toiletries, makeup and personal items are on display in your bathroom and bedrooms. It may sound silly, but a lot of people forget about these items because they are so used to seeing them every day.

Clean Your Home

As simple as it sounds it is extremely important that you clean the whole house including all of the floors, windows, blinds, shutters and bathrooms. Potential buyers will open up built-in drawers and cupboards to look inside, so if possible clean out your drawers and cupboards as well.

When you clean your home you are attracting in positive new energy, this is a great thing to do when you are selling your home. People can notice the difference in the energy of a home that is clean and clear and a home that is tired, dusty and stagnant.

Clear the benchtops in your kitchen, put any excess plates, cups or cutlery away. Try to have a bowl of fresh fruit in your kitchen, a healthy indoor plant or a jar with fresh herb plants in it. If you put a bunch of fresh flowers in a nice vase in your kitchen it will make the space look and smell fantastic.

Pay attention to how your home smells. Use essential oils or scented candles which have soft pleasant scents, you don't want a scent that is too heavy or overpowering.

Intention to Sell

Sometimes one person in a home wants to sell the place but another person doesn't want to move. It is very important that everyone who lives in the home is open and willing to sell.

If someone doesn't want to move or sell it can actually energetically block the home from being sold. If everyone is clear and positive and releases their attachment to the home it will help the home to sell a lot quicker. Try to focus on and look forward to what the sale of your home will do for you, it will open up new beginnings.

Deities, Gods and Goddesses to Call Upon to Sell your Home

Feng Shui is not the only tool that you can use to help you to sell your home quickly. There are many deities, gods and goddesses which you can call upon or pray to who will help you to move forward in your life so that you can sell your home if you want to.

You don't have to be a religious person or be part of a particular faith to call upon these deities. All you need to do is to have a clear and positive intention about what you want to achieve. You also need to be open and grateful and say thank you to the deities, gods or goddesses when you are working with them.

In Hinduism there are some very helpful gods and goddesses such as the Goddess Lakshmi who brings financial abundance, the God Krishna who brings joy and happiness to homes and the Elephant God Ganesh who is the remover of all obstacles. I personally use Ganesh in my everyday life. I take time to think about what obstacles I need to be removed and then I ask Ganesh for help.

When you need to remove any obstacles, say you want to sell your home but it is taking a while, it is a good idea to have a picture of Ganesh on your mobile phone or you can print it out and place it somewhere where you can see it every day.

To ask Ganesh to remove any obstacles you need to ask, in your mind or out loud, the following request "Ganesh, please remove all obstacles so that I can sell my home quickly to the right person for the price that I would like, for the benefit of all and harm to none. Thank you." I always state for the "good of all and harm to none" when I pray or ask for help because I do not want anyone to come to harm as a result of my request. If you do this every day and feel very positive and grateful you will quickly notice some great results. Make sure that you say thank you to any deity that you call upon.

There are many other gods, goddesses and deities that you can call upon or pray to that can help you with abundance or selling your home. It is up to what feels right for you and what your particular beliefs are.

Here is a list of gods, goddesses and deities specifically chosen to help you to sell your home:

Abundantia	Abundance and finances
Archangel Jophiel	Loving thoughts within the family and home and interior decorating
Damara	Abundance, peace and manifesting around the home
Ganesh	Abundance and removing obstacles
Krishna	Joy and happiness to the home
Lakshmi	Space clearing, abundance, beauty, manifesting around the home

In the Catholic faith some people pray to St. Joseph to help them to sell their home. There is a specific prayer to St. Joseph and also a St. Joseph Novena. Here is the prayer to St. Joseph to sell a home:

Prayer to St. Joseph to Sell a Home

O, Saint Joseph, you who taught our Lord the carpenter's trade, and saw to it that he was always properly housed, hear my earnest plea.

I want you to help me now as you helped your foster-child Jesus, and as you have helped many others in the matter of housing.

I wish to sell this property quickly, easily and profitably and I implore you to grant my wish by bringing me a good buyer, one who is eager, compliant and honest, and by letting nothing impede the rapid conclusion of the sale.

Dear Saint Joseph, I know you would do this for me out of the goodness of your heart and in your own good time, but my need is very great now and so I must make you hurry on my behalf.

Saint Joseph, I am going to place you in a difficult position with your head in darkness and you will suffer as our Lord suffered, until this property is sold. Then, Saint Joseph, I swear before the cross and God Almighty, that I will redeem you and you will receive my gratitude and a place of honor in my home. Amen.

The St. Joseph Novena is a prayer which people say for nine days in a row, each day has a different prayer. Many people pray the St. Joseph Novena to pray for what they want specifically, so if you want to sell your home you should have that thought in your mind and really focus upon it and meant it while you say the Novena.

The St. Joseph Novena

Day 1: Oh God, guide of those who listen and helper of those who hear your voice, speak to me, as you did to St. Joseph, and help me accomplish the things you give me to do.

Day 2: Oh God, you love your people and bless the ordinary lives we quietly live. As you blessed St. Joseph, bless what I do, however hidden and simple it may be, and let all I do be done with love.

Day 3: Oh God, ever faithful, you remember us always and in time reveal your blessings. Help me trust in you, as St. Joseph faithfully trusted, and never let me lose faith in the wonderful gifts you promise me.

Day 4: God of families, bless the family that's mine. Keep us safe from harm, and never let evil come between us. Let peace remain in our hearts.

Day 5: Oh God, who loves children, be kind to our children today. Give them eyes of faith for seeing far, a loving heart for welcoming life, and a place always at your side.

Day 6: God of our heavenly home, bless our home on earth. Let the spirit of Mary and Joseph rest at our table, shape our words and actions, and bring blessing to our children.

Day 7: God, our Father, give your fatherly spirit to those who are fathers now. Like Joseph, give them hearts of devoted love for their wives and children and strength for forgiveness and patience.

Day 8: Give shelter, Oh God, to those who need it, and bring together families divided. Give us enough to eat, and decent work to earn our bread. Care for us, Oh God.

Day 9: Bless all families, Oh Lord especially those in need. Remembering the life of your Son, we pray for the poor, for those who lack a good home, for those in exile. Grant them a protector like Joseph, Oh God.
Amen

Some people also believe that it is very helpful to put a St. Joseph medal or statue in the letterbox of the home that they want to sell. Other people believe in burying a St. Joseph statue upside down in the yard of the home that they want to sell as well as saying the St. Joseph prayer or novena.

Each person has their own belief systems so what feels right for some people may not feel right for another person. Stick to what feels right for you, there is no right or wrong way to do things, you may be drawn to a particular deity or you may prefer to focus on manifesting what you want without the deity.

VISION BOARDS

A vision board is a wonderful way for you to focus on what you want to achieve, it is very a very important tool for success because it helps you to remain positive and focused. The positive focused intent helps you to use the law of attraction to attract in what you want.

A vision board is a piece of paper, cardboard or a piece of board where you can make a visual collage of what you want to achieve or attract into your life. Vision boards give you clarity about what it is you want or desire. When you make a vision board you are putting your intent and emotion into it.

You can make your vision board quite simply by writing words on a piece of paper or you may like to create a collage or draw pictures, put photos on the board or cut pictures out of a magazine to stick on the board.

Vision boards make you focus on images and words. When you focus on your vision board you start to manifest and attract in what you want. Because vision boards are used to attract in what you want in life it is important that you be very specific about what it is that you want to attract in. For example if you want to sell your home quickly and for the right price, you can take a photo of your home and stick it on your vision board. You can then write sold across the photo and put a date you want it sold by and a price that you want to sell it for. You may even like to write a statement such as "My house will sell for ___ [add amount] by ___ [add date], this sale will go through smoothly. Both myself and the new owners will be very happy with the outcome of the sale."

A vision board is a very personal thing it is totally up to you what you put on it, it is also up to you whether you hide it in a cupboard or drawer or if you tell anyone about it. Usually you would have the vision board on display where you can see it every day so you can focus upon it. Obviously though if you are selling your home you may have potential buyers and real estate agents looking through your home so you may have to put your vision board away where they can't see it.

Remember the most important thing about a vision board is the intent behind it, focus on what you want to achieve and remain positive.

Ganesh The Elephant God

When you are trying to sell a home it can be incredibly stressful, sometimes all you want to do is sell the home quickly so that you can move on to the new home and start your new way of life. This is how many of my clients have felt over the years when they have come to see me for a reading to ask about when their property will sell. During one of these readings I had a married couple come to me who had almost given up hope on ever selling their home, they had put their home on the market to sell a year earlier and had not had any luck in selling.

During the reading that I provided for them I told them that I saw that they would sell their home within three days, three weeks or three months because I kept being shown a three. I also told them that they both had to want to definitely sell, if one of them was keen to sell but the other one wasn't it wouldn't work. They both looked at each other and the husband admitted that previously he didn't want to move or sell but lately he had wanted to because he saw how important it was to his wife. This made his wife smile. I let them know that this is a great thing that they are now both on the same page wanting to sell.

I also spoke to them about the importance of Feng Shui and how it can make a massive difference to the energy in the home. I gave them a few quick Feng Shui tips and also asked them if they had ever heard about 'Ganesh' The Hindu Elephant God who is the remover of all obstacles. They said no they hadn't heard of him before so I explained to them that they needed to ask Ganesh to please remove all obstacles for the benefit of all and harm to none, so that they can sell their home immediately for the price that they want. They agreed to try this when they got home, I also suggested that they may like to put a picture of Ganesh up on their fridge on in their bedroom to remind themselves to keep positive and to keep asking for the obstacles to be removed.

A few months later I heard back from the married couple, they were very excited because they had just moved into their new home a few weeks earlier. They had sold their home quickly to a young family who was very happy to be moving into the home. After selling their home they bought a small two storey townhouse which they love, so everyone was happy all round. I reminded them to say a big thank you to Ganesh, they promised that they would. It just goes to show you how important it is to have good Feng Shui in your home and to also have the right intent when you are wanting to sell your home.